TUNBRIDGE WELLS AND RUSTHALL COMMONS

A HISTORY AND NATURAL HISTORY

Editor – M.L.J. Rowlands

TUNBRIDGE WELLS MUSEUM AND ART GALLERY

Tunbridge Wells
BOROUGH COUNCIL

Copyright © 2001 Tunbridge Wells Museum and Art Gallery and
Tunbridge Wells Borough Council

ISBN 1-898262-04-7

Published by Tunbridge Wells Museum and Art Gallery

CONTENTS

Illustrations	4
Introduction	8
History of the Commons – I.C. Beavis	12
History of the Manor of Rusthall – R.D.H. Farthing	29
Geology and Palaeontology – E.A. Jarzembowski	48
A New Wealden Fossil Lacewing – E.A. Jarzembowski	56
Animals of the Commons – I.C. Beavis	63
Plants of the Commons – M.W. Page	79
Management of the Commons — S.G. Budden	96
A Tour – I.C. Beavis	109
Bibliography	124

Tunbridge Wells and Rusthall Commons

ILLUSTRATIONS

Black and white pictures appear within the text whilst colour pictures are collected together. The pictures associated with each section are listed below – black and white followed by colour. For pictures of museum exhibits the museum exhibit accession number is given. For pictures from other sources the artist/photographer or source is given.

Cover: *Tunbridge Wells, From Mount Ephraim*, looking across Tunbridge Wells Common. A lithograph by J. Newman, c.1850. 56/67(26)

Introduction
Rocks at Tunbridge Wells. A steel engraving of the St Helena rocks drawn by G. Shepherd and engraved by J. Rolph, 1828. 84/315
Singular Rocks on Rustall Common, near Tunbridge Wells. Kent. A steel engraving by H. Adlard after a drawing by G. Shepherd, c.1828. 84/311e

Vale Royal, London Road, and Tunbridge Wells Common, c.1880. 87/242
A similar view, March 2000. M.L.J. Rowlands

History of the Commons
Bird's-eye view of Tunbridge Wells and the Common. A copper engraving by Jan Kip after a drawing by T. Badslade. Published in 1719 in *The History of Kent* by John Harris. 56/67(34)
Vote Against the Bad Bargain, a Commons campaign poster of Thomas Edwards, 1889. 1973/06(158)

Rocks at Tunbridge Wells. A watercolour of the St Helena caves and London Road by James Lambert, 1786. 59/09(1)
The Pantiles viewed from Bath Square, c.1860. 87/251
A similar view, December 2000. M.L.J. Rowlands
Brighton Lake, Eridge Road, c.1903. Photograph by J. Welch, with, from left to right, Mrs Jessie and Lilian Kember and Mrs and Dorothy Welch. 89/210
A similar view, April 2000. M.L.J. Rowlands
Royal Victoria Grove, c.1912. 97/317
A similar view, October 2000. M.L.J. Rowlands

History of the Manor of Rusthall
Thomas Neale Esq. depicted on a medal of 1694. The British Museum
Pencil sketch of Castle Cottage and Castle Road by J.J. Dodd (1810-94),

A History and Natural History

from the Winsch Album
The Bath House, the Pantiles. Engraved by Letitia Byrne after a drawing by Paul Amsinck. From Amsinck 1810. 81/222
Diana Menuhin and Griselda Kentner attend the Tunbridge Wells 350th anniversary celebrations at the Pantiles, September 1956
The Honourable Jeremy Menuhin
Pedigree – Sir George Kelley to the Present Day

The Pantiles, Tunbridge Wells. Thomas Loggan's gouache painting of the northern end of the Pantiles showing the enclosure and archway erected by Charles Muskerry, c.1740. The British Museum
Watercolour of George Kelley's house at Bishops Down, late eighteenth-century. 84/678
Manor portraits. Both appear to be those attributed to Angelica Kaufmann by Rosamund Suart. They may be George Kelley and Ann Gardner. Private collection

Geology and Palaeontology
Reconstruction drawing of an *Iguanodon*. Philip Eglise
Toad Rock and Rusthall, c.1913. 58/84(15)
A similar view, March 2000. M.L.J. Rowlands

The Parson's Nose Rock. A watercolour by Charles Tattershall Dodd, c.1840. 90/237
Denny Bottom and the Loaf Rock, c.1880. 63/48
A similar view, March 2000. M.L.J. Rowlands
Wellington Rocks and the Wellington Hotel, c.1905. 81/260
A similar view, March 2000. M.L.J. Rowlands

A New Wealden Fossil Lacewing
Venation and colour pattern of *Kalligramma roycrowsoni* sp. nov., unique type. Scale line = 1 mm. From Jarzembowski 1987
Restoration drawing of *Kalligramma roycrowsoni* sp. nov. in flight. Neil Watson

Animals of the Commons
Nest and eggs of a Linnet on Tunbridge Wells Common. A photograph by Harold Betteridge from his 1962-4 Tunbridge Wells Common album. 75/43(37)
Nest and eggs of a Nightingale on Tunbridge Wells Common. A photograph by Harold Betteridge from his 1962-4 Tunbridge Wells Common album. 75/43(37)

Tunbridge Wells and Rusthall Commons

Hoverfly *Volucella pellucens*. I.C. Beavis
Swallow-tailed Moth. I.C. Beavis
Flower beetle *Oedemera nobilis*. I.C. Beavis
Peacock butterfly. I.C. Beavis
Small Tortoiseshell butterfly. I.C. Beavis
Female Common Blue butterfly. I.C. Beavis
Azure Damselfly. I.C. Beavis
Nomad bee *Nomada goodeniana*. I.C. Beavis

Plants of the Commons
Wild Arum. H.S. Page
Harebell. H.S. Page
Water Crowfoot. H.S. Page
Common Dog Violet. H.S. Page
Buckshorn Plantain. H.S. Page

Crab apple. H.S. Page
Ragwort. H.S. Page
Coral Root. From Forster's *Flora Tonbrigensis* (1842)
Hogweed. H.S. Page
Ragged Robin. H.S. Page
Rosebay. H.S. Page

Management of the Commons
View towards Mount Edgcumbe from above Gibraltar, *c.*1890. 89/154
A similar view, March 2000. M.L.J. Rowlands
View across the Common towards Mount Ephraim, *c.*1905. 81/266
A similar view, March 2000. M.L.J. Rowlands

Rusthall Common photographed by George Glanville, from his album of 1884. 81/253
Watercolour by Alfred Robert Quinton of the Common from Mount Ephraim, *c.*1912. 96/636
Bracken Cottage Pond after restoration. S.G. Budden
Mount Edgcumbe Rocks, partially cleared. S.G. Budden
Mount Edgcumbe Rocks during clearing in the winter of 1994-5. S.G. Budden
Mount Edgcumbe Rocks after clearing. S.G. Budden

A Tour
Donkey Boys on the Common. A photograph by Percy Lankester, *c.*1890. 87/236
Tunbridge Wells. A view of Queen Anne's Grove. A steel engraving by

A History and Natural History

H. Adlard after a drawing by George Shepherd, 1828. 87/92
The Common Tunbridge Wells. A watercolour by John Preston Neale of the south-western corner of Tunbridge Wells Common looking toward Ropers Gate, 1847. 95/221
Air raid shelter in the caves beneath St Helena. A drawing by E. Owen Jennings, April 1941. 73/97
Tunbridge Wells, from the Race-Course. A wood engraving of *c.*1850. 56/68(71)

Fir Tree Pond and Major York's Road, *c.*1905. 58/11(5)
A similar view, March 2000. M.L.J. Rowlands
Sketch map of Tunbridge Wells Common. I.C. Beavis
Sketch map of Rusthall Common. I.C. Beavis
Sketch map of Denny Bottom. I.C. Beavis

Tunbridge Wells and Rusthall Commons

INTRODUCTION

To the broad range of people who pass through, around, or by Tunbridge Wells and Rusthall Commons, or who 'use' them, their significance is equally wide. The Commons are at least an oasis of apparent countryside projecting right into the centre of Tunbridge Wells. But they are also places to play cricket, places to jog, places to climb rock outcrops, places to walk the dog, places to hunt for insects, and so on. To natural historians they have a diverse flora and fauna including several rare species and a Site of Special Scientific Interest. As well as a long prehistory of rock formation and roaming dinosaurs, the Commons' recorded human history stretches back to medieval times; the past two centuries spiced with disputes over ownership, rights, and management. This book draws together essays from five local experts in their fields to cover fully the highlights of the Commons' history and natural history. The contributors are Ian Beavis, Museum Officer (Local and Natural History) at Tunbridge Wells Museum; Steve Budden, Warden to the Commons Conservators; Roger Farthing, Tunbridge Wells local historian; Ed Jarzembowski, Keeper of Natural History at Maidstone Museum and Bentlif Art Gallery; and local botanist Mary Page.

The first essay, by Ian Beavis, is a general history of the Commons beginning with the earliest known records in medieval times. Here we see how a dispute in the early 1700s resulted in an Act of Parliament which has caused the preservation of the Commons in their largely undeveloped form ever since. Many towns have commons – often as minute patches of land which are manicured lawns devoid of features and which one can walk across in less than two minutes – but how many of these commons have diverse habitats, vistas, unusual natural features, and spread to over 250 acres?

A résumé of the descent of the Manor of Rusthall is covered in Roger Farthing's essay. Although ownership of the Manor, and thus the freehold of the Commons, changed hands several times in the Middle Ages, since the early 1700s the descent has been through one family. Due to a chronic lack of male heirs the Lordship frequently passed between daughters and cousins, hence the Lord's surname changed frequently. For the past few decades the surname has been a well-known one – but not well known due to the Manor connection. Today the Lord of the Manor of Rusthall is the Honourable Jeremy Menuhin.

Many millions of years of history and natural history are described in the geology and palaeontology essay. This includes an account of the geological structure of the Weald and its origin, Wealden fossils, and the prominent rock outcrops of the Commons. Ed Jarzembowski also gives a name for the first time to a unique and hitherto anonymous Wealden fossil lacewing – the most

A History and Natural History

common modern lacewings being delicate insects with long clear wings and a body and wing veins in a pale shade of green. This new species is based upon a fossilized fragment of an insect's wing, examination of which showed the insect to be of a species not recognized before, and thus needing its own name.

The fossil lacewing is named after Roy Crowson, a distinguished scientist and a leading researcher in the systematics of beetles, who in his early years was a curator at Tunbridge Wells Museum. After graduating from the Imperial College of Science and Technology, Roy served until World War II as assistant curator at the Museum. A committee minute of the Borough Council records that in a meeting on 21 September 1944 a proposal was made for an increase in the salary of 'Mr. R.A. Crowson, Assistant Curator, Borough Museum, . . . in the event of his release from the Royal Air Force.' He did return but moved in 1948 to Scotland to take up a lectureship in taxonomy at the University of Glasgow. A prolific author, Roy published over 200 works, mostly on aspects of the biology and taxonomy of beetles. He began in 1938 with an article titled 'The metendosternite in Coleoptera' for the *Transactions of the Royal Entomological Society* (Pakaluk 1995). Although he wrote much afterwards, his magnum opus came in 1981 with *The Biology of the Coleoptera*, a book which is a classic in the field. In 1980 the Linnean Society awarded Roy their Linnean Medal for Zoology in recognition of his contribution to the field of entomology. Also, at least thirteen other types of animal have been named in honour of Roy, from the genus *Crowsonius* to the species *Lapethus crowsoni*. Roy Crowson died on 13 May 1999, aged eighty-four years.

After the naming of the new fossil, Ian Beavis and Mary Page write on the wide variety of plant and animal life of the Commons. Although projecting into the centre of town, to the west the Commons are adjacent to open countryside. This continues to allow migration of species which would not be viable were the Commons an island literally in the centre of town. Although common plant and animal species abound, the Commons enjoy a number of uncommon or even rare species including Purple Hairstreak butterflies, White-legged Damselflies, Coral Root, Solomon's Seal, and the Royal Fern.

The gradual cessation of grazing and, to a certain extent, relaxed management in the middle decades of the twentieth century, allowed both Commons to move towards a natural state not seen there for centuries. Gradually trees began to replace gorse, heather, and bracken, undergrowth obscured rock formations, and panoramic views were lost. Throughout this book selected Museum illustrations of the Commons of around 1900 and before are paired with specially taken modern photographs of the same views to demonstrate the differences over a century. Generally, the man-made features (e.g. the Pantiles) seem to have changed little, but elsewhere an advancing

Tunbridge Wells and Rusthall Commons

Rocks at Tunbridge Wells. A steel engraving of the St Helena rocks drawn by G. Shepherd and engraved by J. Rolph, 1828.

Singular Rocks on Rustall Common, near Tunbridge Wells. Kent. A steel engraving by H. Adlard after a drawing by G. Shepherd, *c.*1828.

A History and Natural History

force of trees seems to have invaded everywhere that used to have the appearance of a moor. The devastation of the Great Storm of 1987 became a catalyst for broader policies on management of the entire Commons. Reassessment of the Commons resulted in a new management plan by which chosen areas are being restored to their condition of a century ago. It would be impractical to restore the entire Commons faithfully to their early twentieth-century state – not least because in some areas the panoramic views now would look over twentieth-century building projects rather than attractive natural topography. Instead, selected ponds are being restored, trees removed, rock outcrops re-exposed, and undergrowth cleared, which will result, perhaps more than it was a century ago, in diverse natural habitats, viewpoints and features. Steve Budden's essay explains how he and his colleagues are putting into effect the management plan.

Matched with three sketch maps of the Commons, the concluding essay gives a tour of the Commons, pointing out both the interesting natural and man-made features.

Some of the essays refer to information sources and suggested further reading. In Roger Farthing's essay superscript numbers in the text refer to a Notes section immediately at the end of his text. The Notes give additional information or refer to unpublished information sources in various archives. In other instances, authors' references to published works are noted in the text in the form Author, Year. A bibliography is placed at the end of the book where all published references are listed by author in alphabetical order.

There are a number of people to whom we acknowledge our thanks for their contributions to this publication. Without the contributing authors there would be no book. All of these also contributed illustrations. Other pictures came from Philip Eglise (the *Iguanodon* reconstruction), Harold Page (drawings and photographs of Commons plants), Neil Watson (a drawing of the new species of *Kalligramma* in flight), and Jeremy Menuhin. The Trustees of the British Museum allowed reproduction of the medal depicting Thomas Neale and Loggan's gouache of the Pantiles, whilst J. Salmon Ltd. allowed use of the A.R. Quinton watercolour. The owner of the two Manor portraits kindly allowed them to be used. To all of these contributors we are grateful. Dr J.D. Radley kindly proofread Ed Jarzembowski's text.

Tunbridge Wells and Rusthall Commons

HISTORY OF THE COMMONS
Ian Beavis

The earliest known inhabitants of what are now the Commons were the Mesolithic hunter gatherers of *c.*4500 BC who led a nomadic lifestyle and employed the various rock outcrops in the Tunbridge Wells area as regular encampment sites. The rocks were prominent landmarks in the vast Wealden forest, and their sandstone cliffs had convenient overhangs which could be used to provide shelter and protection. These people probably encouraged the development of heathland in the vicinity of the rocks by maintaining open areas through burning in order to attract grazing deer. The characteristic flint implements of the Mesolithic period have been found on Rusthall Common, near the rocks at Happy Valley and Denny Bottom.

The Commons first emerge into recorded history in Saxon times, when the earliest known mention of Rusthall occurs in a charter of AD 765 in which Egbert king of Kent grants to Diora bishop of Rochester property at Halling along with its associated swine pastures including Speldhurst and Rustwell. The old spelling 'Rustwell' is thought to refer to the chalybeate springs in the area (even the famous Pantiles spring was originally on the Common). Swine pastures were carved out of the Wealden forest in considerable numbers from the fifth century onwards and were known as dens. Bishops Down, the ancient name of Tunbridge Wells Common may originally have been Bishops Den. Such pastures were in use for about seven weeks in the autumn when pigs were driven onto them from the settled areas north of the forest to be fattened for slaughter by feeding on acorns and beech mast.

Over the years these forest pastures gradually began to attract a permanent population, and many developed into the Wealden towns and villages of today. But although there was some settlement at Rusthall it never grew into anything large enough to be dignified with the name of a village. Until the development of Tunbridge Wells as a spa resort, it remained no more than a scattering of dwellings in an outlying corner of Speldhurst parish. With settlement would have come more extensive clearance of tree cover and the spread of heathland vegetation over a much wider area. Before the development of the Pantiles in the late seventeenth century, the Common was continuous with the heathland of Waterdown Forest, the landscape of the future town being described in 1656 as 'a valley compassed about with stony hills, so barren, that there groweth nothing but heath upon the same'.

By the medieval period, Rusthall had become a manor, with a Lord, Freeholders, and Wastes. The Freeholders or Freehold Tenants were inhabitants who had been granted portions of land within the Manor boundaries by the Lord in perpetuity, although still owing certain feudal dues. The Wastes

A History and Natural History

of the Manor, which we know today as the two Commons, were available to the Freeholders for grazing their animals and as a source of what was later described as 'marl, stone, sand, loam, mould, gravel or clay' as well as 'furze, gorse or litter'.

In 1606 Dudley Lord North, in poor health due to over-indulgence at Court, was staying at Eridge Castle with Lord Abergavenny, whose estate was contiguous with the Manor of Rusthall. While riding along what we now know as Eridge Road, he spotted some orange coloured water on the edge of the Common which he recognized as coming from a chalybeate (iron bearing) spring similar to those at Spa in Belgium which were already famous for their supposed health giving properties. Subsequently, Lord North began to drink the spring water regularly and claimed that it restored him to perfect health. News of the discovery spread rapidly and in 1608 Lord Abergavenny obtained permission from the Lord of the Manor to sink the first well on the site for the convenience of visitors.

In 1664 Lord Muskerry, having acquired the Manor of Rusthall, improved access to the spring by building a new enclosure with an ornamental arch. In 1682 his widow sold the Manor to Thomas Neale who negotiated an agreement with the Freeholders allowing him to build shops, lodgings and other facilities for visitors on a strip of the Common adjacent to the spring. After a fire in 1687, he constructed the colonnade which we now know as the Pantiles. The Freeholders received an annual payment in compensation for loss of grazing rights. In 1732, by which time the Manor had changed hands twice, a lawsuit broke out between Maurice Conyers, the new Lord, and the Freeholders over the question of continued compensation after Neale's original agreement had expired. The Freeholders were successful in asserting their rights over the Pantiles site, and the resulting settlement was embodied in the Rusthall Manor Act of 1739.

Although the 1739 Act was primarily concerned with dividing ownership of the Pantiles between the Lord and the Freeholders, it also legislated against further encroachment on the Commons without the mutual consent of both parties and thus provided a solid legal foundation for their survival as an open space to the present day. In earlier times, manorial courts had attempted to control the problem of unauthorized building on the Commons, but with limited success. Working buildings, as opposed to dwellings, were given retrospective permission in some instances. In other cases fines were imposed on offenders, but the buildings involved remained in place. John Bowra's map of 1738, produced in connection with the Rusthall Manor Act, shows a number of encroachments on Tunbridge Wells Common that had become established by that date. There are two forges overlooking London Road, two lodging houses and a cottage on Mount Edgcumbe, and some buildings on the triangular

Tunbridge Wells and Rusthall Commons

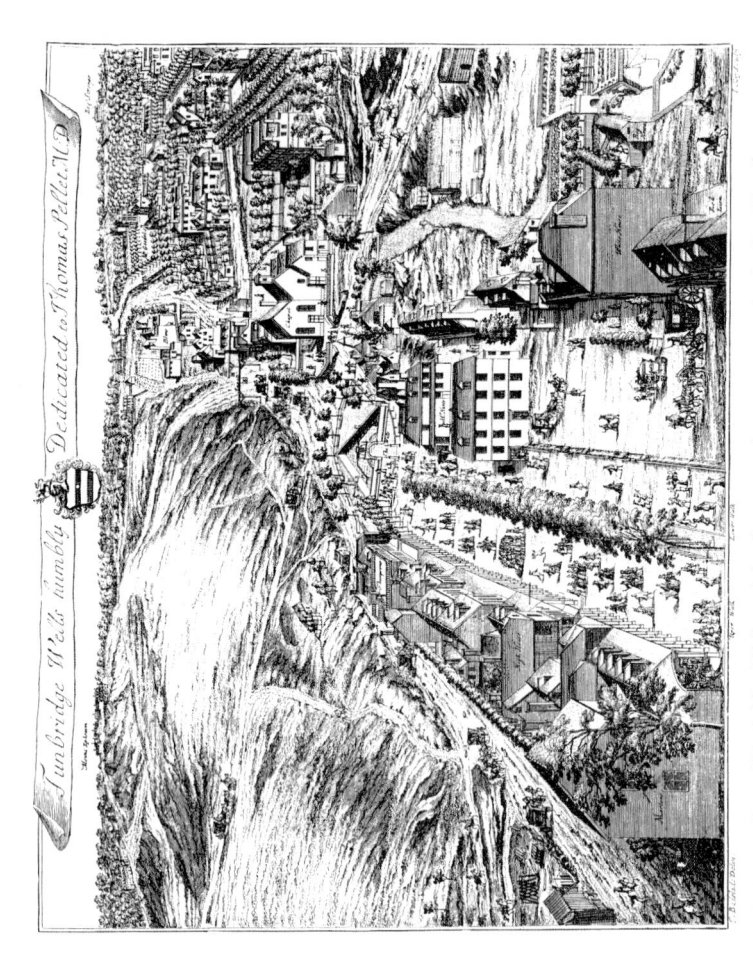

Bird's-eye view of Tunbridge Wells and the Common. A copper engraving by Jan Kip after a drawing by T. Badslade. Published in 1719 in *The History of Kent* by John Harris.

A History and Natural History

portion of the Common where London Road and Mount Ephraim meet. The latter probably began as workmens' sheds associated with the quarrying of stone and sand from the rock outcrops on the site, gradually evolving into permanent dwellings.

As Tunbridge Wells developed as a fashionable holiday resort, the Commons came to be perceived as more than a purely functional landscape, since they provided a picturesque backdrop to the organized amusements provided for the benefit of visitors. The original Assembly Room for public entertainments was established in 1655 on Rusthall Common, with an adjacent bowling green, since due to lack of accommodation near the chalybeate spring many lodged in the vicinity. Although these facilities were moved to Mount Ephraim a decade later, Rusthall remained of sufficient importance for a cold bath and associated pleasure grounds to be opened in 1708 in the area later known as Happy Valley. Some eighteenth-century residents and visitors believed that the Commons would benefit from tree planting and other embellishments, but the planting of Queen Anne's Grove in 1702 (along with Queen Anne's Oak a couple of years earlier) is the only reported example prior to 1835. A race course was established on Tunbridge Wells Common from an early date, and in 1801 the popular pastime of donkey riding was introduced. Clifford's Tunbridge Wells guide (1818) reports that 'The Common, on which are walks, rides, romantic rocks, the race ground, &c. has become a favourite place of resort with the visitors to the Wells. The turf is covered, during the summer, with flocks of sheep; and pedestrians, equestrians, and asinurians, of all ranks, sexes and ages amuse themselves on it'. In a subsequent edition (1823) he encourages his readers to explore Rusthall Common, where 'the views over various parts of Kent and Sussex are the most delightful and extensive' and the rocks are 'very remarkable for the singular shapes which many of them present'.

By the beginning of the nineteenth century, the management of the Commons was in the hands of the Freeholders, who were responsible for regulating the use of the Commons for grazing and other purposes, collecting rents for permitted encroachments, and general management such as maintaining ponds and drainage channels. The growing population of the town put increasing pressure on the Commons, and the Freeholders began to realize that some active policing was necessary in order to 'check the many trespasses and depredations that are constantly committed'. As well as the old problems of unauthorized encroachment, they now had to contend with dumping of rubbish, firing of the gorse, extensive destruction of the soil by persons digging for marl and sand, and over-grazing. It was discovered that local residents were acquiring tiny pieces of land within the manor boundaries so that they could claim the right to pasture large numbers of animals on the

Tunbridge Wells and Rusthall Commons

Commons, greatly outnumbering those of the legitimate Freeholders. In 1824 the Freeholders formed a committee to act as executive between their annual meetings, and from 1827 they began to employ a Common Driver and Pound Keeper to oversee the Commons on a day-to-day basis.

When John Colbran published his *New Guide for Tunbridge Wells* in 1839, the new regime had made the Commons much more well-ordered, the Freeholders executing 'very summary justice on those who attempt to invade their rights'. It is Colbran who tells us how the Freeholders, on account of their enthusiastic tackling of abuses, had acquired the nickname of Hogpounders, a term which 'although originally applied in derision, is now rather courted than rejected by them'. It alluded to the impounding of offending animals, which were not returned to the owner until a fine had been paid. At their annual meeting the Freeholders used to perambulate the manor, inspecting any unauthorized buildings or fences, after which they held a dinner known as the 'Hogpounders' Feast'. Colbran, himself a Freeholder, is keen to remind his readers of their public spirited attitude, describing them as 'a body of men to whom the visitors and inhabitants of the Wells are greatly indebted, inasmuch as they are the means of protecting the beautiful Commons'. In 1861 the Freeholders decided that their role as guardians of the Commons required some legal backing. With the support of the Manor they sought a new Act of Parliament to supplement the legislation of 1739. The result of their efforts was the Rusthall Manor Act of 1863, which established a formal register of Freeholders and empowered the Freeholders' Committee to make by-laws.

The policy of the Freeholders was not in fact entirely altruistic. As well as protecting their own grazing and other rights, many of them were tradesmen and lodging house keepers and so had an interest in maintaining the Commons as an attraction for visitors. The first deliberate attempts to beautify the Commons (apart from the 1700-02 plantings) took place in this period, beginning with the planting of Royal Victoria Grove in 1835 to commemorate the visits of the young Princess Victoria (who had greatly enjoyed her rides on the Common on her donkey called Flower), and to supersede the dying Queen Anne's Grove. In 1858 representatives of the Freeholders met with Revd William Law Pope's Poor Fund Committee, set up to provide work for unemployed labourers. They agreed upon a programme of works which included the creation from a swampy hollow of what is now known as Brighton Lake, and the levelling of a 'greensward terrace walk' running parallel with Eridge Road on the slope above the new lake. In 1867 the Freeholders agreed to collaborate with the Tradesmen's Association in planting trees on various parts of Tunbridge Wells Common, whose open heathy landscape appeared to many to be somewhat barren. The newly formed Association for Promoting the Interests of the Town of Tunbridge Wells approached the Freeholders in

A History and Natural History

1874 with a scheme to create a turf walk or Promenade on the top of the Common along Mount Ephraim. This was finally put into effect in 1881, providing a pleasant stroll for fashionable visitors, from which they could obtain panoramic views of the town.

The last decade of the Freeholders' supremacy over the Commons was marked by controversy, beginning in 1882 with claims on the part of the Local Board (the town's original government) and other prominent townsfolk that the Freeholders were becoming too lax in permitting encroachments. There had long been a practice of permitting the occupiers of property on or adjacent to the Commons to take over small portions of land on payment of an annual rent, but now there were requests for larger enclosures. This resulted from the fact that the dwellings situated on the Commons originally owned only the land on which they stood. This had not been a problem when they were mere workmen's cottages, but when they were rebuilt as desirable Victorian residences the owners became unhappy that the general public had a right to walk up to their property and peer through their windows.

The most heavily criticized incident occurred when the Freeholders' Committee gave permission to the occupier of St Helena Cottage to 'enclose a portion of the rocks and Common with an iron fence'. The Local Board protested that 'the recent enclosures and obstructions were illegal', while local solicitor Frank William Stone, along with his brother Frederick, launched a personal campaign to change the Freeholders' policy. The brothers owned land within the Manor boundary and so were entitled to register as Freeholders. Gathering together sixteen eligible supporters (including the Tunbridge ware maker Thomas Barton), they submitted their names to the Freeholders' Committee in October 1882. Initially there was resistance, the meeting resolving that 'the claims of the above . . . have not been made out to the satisfaction of the Committee'. Several of the campaigners appeared at the annual meeting of the Freeholders a month later, but were ejected.

By the time of their meeting in February 1883, the Freeholders' Committee had been forced to concede that there was no legal reason to exclude the eighteen new applicants, and they were registered without further argument. In May a further list of twenty names was submitted and accepted, including prominent members of the Local Board. The newcomers now had a clear majority over their opponents, and the stage was set for a takeover of the Freeholders' Committee. The Freeholders' Annual Meeting in November 1883 was a stormy affair at which the chairman John Stone Wigg (later the town's first mayor) had considerable difficulty keeping order. Frank Stone's supporters arrived in force and succeeded in electing an entirely new Committee from among their number. The vote was greeted by shouts of protest from the opposition, who tried to argue that it was technically invalid,

Tunbridge Wells and Rusthall Commons

but the chairman overruled them. A vote was also carried to the effect that 'all obstructions, posts and rails, and chain fencing between Onslow House and Romanoff Lodge and Mount Edgcumbe House be forthwith removed'.

In later years Frank Stone was credited with 'saving the Commons', which was doubtless an exaggeration, but the election of the new Committee did mark a return to the stricter policy of earlier times. However, what were seen as positive developments were not ruled out. In 1885-6 the Lower Cricket Ground was levelled to relieve pressure on the older ground on Tunbridge Wells Common, and Rusthall Common was provided with a formal cricket ground for the first time. The Lower Cricket Ground had earlier been used informally as a playing field by the boys of Romanoff House School in London Road, and it was also the site of the annual bonfire on November 5th which the Freeholders had permitted since 1860 in an effort to eliminate the traditional custom of indiscriminate firing of the gorse bushes. In 1886 a scheme was brought forward to purchase the old forge and associated buildings at Fonthill, to demolish them, and to return the land to the open Common, but due to the change of administration four years later the project was never brought to completion.

The present system of managing the Commons, under a body of twelve Conservators, was established by the Tunbridge Wells Improvement Act of 1890, a lengthy piece of legislation which laid down the powers and responsibilities of the new Borough Council established in the previous year, and which contained a thirteen page section on the Commons. The history of the Act, and particularly the provisions relating to the Commons, is complex. The parliamentary process was originally set in motion by the old Local Board, one of whose prime objectives was to gain as much control as possible over the management of the Commons, as they had been frustrated by their impotence in the affair of the enclosure of St Helena. The Manor and Freeholders, who felt strongly that they had managed the Commons perfectly satisfactorily since time immemorial, objected to the Board's ambitions and petitioned Parliament in opposition to the original version of the Bill. Negotiations were opened between the three parties, and eventually a compromise was reached establishing that the Conservators should consist of four persons each appointed by the Manor, the Freeholders, and the Council, with the duty to 'maintain the Commons free from all encroachments'. Accompanying the Act was the first definitive map of the boundaries of the Commons, with the permitted encroachments to date. The Conservators now took over the day to day management of the Commons from the Freeholders' Committee, as well as the power to frame by-laws. The Act also stated explicitly for the first time that 'the inhabitants of Tunbridge Wells and the neighbourhood shall have free access'. Although the 1890 Act as a whole is

A History and Natural History

FELLOW BURGESSES,
OUR COMMONS,
VOTE AGAINST
THE
BAD BARGAIN

About to be made by the Town with the Lord of the Manor & Freeholders.

Why, what have they conceded to the Town? The right to send 4 Councillors as Conservators to attend their Meetings to be out-voted by their 8 Conservators----a hopeless minority.

It is also hampered by

UNNECESSARY RESTRICTIONS & FINES.

WHY SPEND SUCH A LARGE SUM OF MONEY FOR SUCH A

Paltry Concession ?

IT IS A BAD BARGAIN - VOTE AGAINST IT

AND THROW IT OUT.

THOMAS EDWARDS,
Salem, Tunbridge Wells,
A Native and an Old Inhabitant.   Dec. 9, 1889.

J. H. CANE, PRINTER, 69A, CAMDEN ROAD, TUNBRIDGE WELLS.

Vote Against the Bad Bargain, a Commons campaign poster of Thomas Edwards, 1889.

Tunbridge Wells and Rusthall Commons

no longer in operation, its essential provisions relating to the Commons were re-enacted in the County of Kent Act of 1981.

In the late Victorian and Edwardian period, the Commons were probably to be seen at their best. They were much frequented by residents and visitors, as can be seen from the numerous postcard views entitled 'Sunday Afternoon on the Common' which depict crowds sitting on the grassy slopes overlooking London Road. The old problems of digging and quarrying that made parts of the Commons unsightly, and of excessive numbers of grazing animals, had now come to an end. As belief in the efficacy of the Pantiles spring declined, so the town's claim to be a health resort began to be focussed on the local environment in general, with walks on the breezy Commons being highly recommended to promote recovery from sickness. According to the 1903 town guide, 'On the hottest day in summer there is always a cool, scent laden breeze, sweeping over the glorious Common, and to breathe this air is to take in new life and enjoy a feeling of stimulated vitality and buoyancy such as only a pure and salubrious atmosphere and pleasant surroundings can arouse'.

At the same time, the natural vegetation of the Commons began to be appreciated by the public in general as well as by the dedicated botanist. Pelton's guide, constantly reprinted from 1871 to the beginning of the new century, contains a characteristic description: 'To our modern taste its natural and wild condition renders it far more attractive than the artificial parks which it is the fashion to provide for the healthful recreation of the dwellers in large cities. The furze bushes and the brake are the most noticeable ornaments; but the whole expanse abounds with other plants and blossoms – ling and heath, chamomile and thyme, milkwort and wild violets, being among the most abundant. In April and May the golden bloom of the furze, which is unusually profuse in this spot, delights the eye, and its rich perfume scents the breeze'.

The practise of large scale tree planting, begun under the management of the Freeholders, was continued by the Conservators. The general view was that additional trees served to enhance the natural beauties of the Commons. In 1895 the Tradesmen's Association, who with their interest in promoting tourism maintained a keen interest in the Commons, organized a scheme whereby individuals and organizations could contribute one or more trees, and about 150 were planted over the course of a week in November. The new and outgoing mayors, Major Fletcher Lutwidge and Sir David Salomons, ceremonially performed the first plantings beside Major York's Road. What was not anticipated was that as these trees matured and grazing declined they would begin to seed themselves all over the Commons, beginning a process of uncontrolled transformation of heathland to woodland.

In 1931 C.H. Strange gave a lecture to the Tunbridge Wells Natural History Society, in which he related the history of commemorative tree planting on

A History and Natural History

the Commons, including the most recent examples (near Highbury and leading up to Rusthall Church) to mark the accession and coronation of George V. But he concluded by warning that the number of trees was becoming excessive. 'If there is to be any further tree-planting on the Common', he said, 'it is hoped that it will be done with circumspection and foresight. I am inclined to think we have almost enough forest trees. It is a fact that the view from Mount Ephraim, an ever lovely panorama of moorland, field and forest, is becoming more and more intercepted by growing trees. Above all, we ought to aim at a better care and cultivation of the trees we already possess; that they may be protected from injury, cut down and replaced where decayed, and those that are neither useful for shade nor ornamental to look at should be removed'. However, further commemorative planting did take place in 1935, to celebrate George V's silver jubilee, and on a larger scale for the coronation of George VI in 1937. In the latter year, the 'King's Avenue' of flowering cherries was created along the Donkey Drive (Mount Edgcumbe Road), along with the 'King's Grove' south of Mount Edgcumbe (later swamped by invading scrub).

Meanwhile, the Chamber of Trade (incorporating the old Tradesmen's Association) had also noticed that all was not well on the Commons. In a report presented to the Conservators in the same year as Strange's lecture, they pointed out that an excessive number of young trees, in particular birches, were springing up, that ponds were silting up, and that the traditional heathland vegetation was diminishing. In subsequent years several prominent local residents complained about problems such as the invasion of bracken and the fact that heather was 'rapidly disappearing'. No one seems to have realized that the immediate cause of these changes was the decline in grazing, which had ceased altogether by the outbreak of World War II. Wartime conditions then disrupted the management of the Commons, causing unavoidable neglect. Any effective action that the Conservators might otherwise have taken was prevented, not only by a shortage of manpower but also by various military and civil defence activities on the Commons themselves.

As early as 1938, some of the town's first air raid shelters appeared in the form of open trenches on Tunbridge Wells Common, while in October 1939 the Borough Council was authorized to convert the caves under St Helena Cottage into more permanent shelters. By December 1940 there were already four bomb craters on the two Commons, including one in the middle of the Higher Cricket Ground. In 1941 large scale clearance of gorse bushes and other vegetation was undertaken in order to avoid the risk of fires caused by incendiary bombs. Such fires, it was thought, would not only endanger houses on and around the Commons, but would also 'serve as a beacon lighting up the town for a further enemy attack'.

In 1942 further works were carried out. A reinforced concrete shelter was

Tunbridge Wells and Rusthall Commons

constructed by Brighton Lake, and the National Fire Service constructed three steel tanks on concrete bases, two on Tunbridge Wells and one on Rusthall Common, each holding 23,000 gallons of water. In the same year, the railings around the two cricket grounds were removed for the war effort. By this time, several pieces of land on both Commons had been requisitioned by the military for purposes which included the siting of anti-aircraft guns and searchlight emplacements. The Conservators complained vigorously about the hazards caused by the widespread presence of entrenchments and other concealed excavations, especially when a local resident was injured by falling into an unprotected gun pit.

Although the military authorities paid compensation for actual damage to the Commons, and it was reported that almost all damage had been made good by 1946, general neglect leading to uncontrolled growth of vegetation did not prove so easy to reverse. The absence of sheep and cattle left the task of keeping back scrub and bracken to human activity alone, but labour to perform the necessary work was in short supply. The desirability of reintroducing grazing was debated by the Conservators in the late 1940s, but clearly no way of achieving this could be found. In 1947, the occupant of the cottage at Bull's Hollow complained to the Conservators that 'seedlings had grown into trees and her premises were now enclosed in a tangle of bracken, trees and weeds', only to be told that 'owing to shortage of labour it had not been possible to effect the clearance of undergrowth'. In the following year, the Freehold Tenants made more general observations on 'the present unsatisfactory state of the Commons', but received a similar answer.

On the day of Elizabeth II's coronation in 1953, Tunbridge Wells Common fulfilled its traditional role as a scene for local celebrations. These were centred on the Higher Cricket Ground, where 'a great crowd assembled for the fancy dress parade, to hear the Queen's message broadcast, to see a firework display and the bonfire lit, and to take part in community singing'. There was also, as on previous royal occasions, a tree planting ceremony, in this case involving two flowering cherries placed by the Mayor and Deputy Mayor on either side of the cricket pavilion.

Meanwhile, the Conservators were fighting what seemed to be a losing battle against rampant saplings and bracken. In the mid-1950s we find them discussing the fact that 'sycamore and silver birch trees were becoming too prolific' and instructing the Surveyor 'to report as to the action which may be taken to restrict the spread of bracken'. However, as memory of the Commons' original condition faded, it became increasingly difficult to formulate a coherent policy or define a vision of what kind of landscape the Commons should be.

In 1957, H.G. Tucker, the Surveyor, carried out a detailed survey of the

A History and Natural History

two Commons and offered proposals for their restoration. However, these now took for granted that the Commons consisted largely of woodland, and failed to address the question of vanished heath and grassland. The results were contradictory. Some saplings of unwanted species were eliminated, but at the same time 269 fresh saplings, mainly oak, were planted. The Race Course was cleared, and there was much talk about removal of undergrowth. But what this consisted of was no more than a 'policy of clearing undergrowth and small defective trees alongside roads and footpaths'. The possibility of grazing by goats was actively considered, while an active policy of exterminating rabbits was pursued. No one appreciated that rabbits helped to maintain open grassland.

During the 1960s management of the Commons had clearly become a holding operation, designed simply to stabilize what was perceived to be their natural condition. Radical intervention was no longer considered. This situation was epitomized by the case of the Happy Valley viewpoint, which was under discussion throughout the decade. When it was first reported in 1961 that the view so much admired by the Victorians and Edwardians was now invisible due to obscuring vegetation, the Surveyor proceeded to order the removal of 'dead and dying holly trees and relatively small and poorly shaped oak trees'. The same type of work was carried out in 1967, but by the following year residents of Rusthall were still complaining that the view could not be seen. Two years later, similar arguments began over the condition of Toad Rock.

By the 1970s the originally open character of the Commons had been almost entirely transformed. Increasing numbers of self-sown trees, along with a spread of bracken and bramble, had produced a landscape that for the most part appeared to be woodland traversed by narrow footpaths. The Race Course had become a forest ride. Heathland had been virtually extinguished, surviving only in a few dwindling patches which were being steadily encroached upon by taller undergrowth. The once ubiquitous gorse bushes flourished only in a few open spots, while elsewhere they were being shaded out by the tree canopy. Acid grassland still survived on the northern and southern fringes of Tunbridge Wells Common, but it was clearly threatened by advancing woodland. Victorian seats hemmed in by vegetation hinted at lost viewpoints. Some rock formations, notably at Mount Edgcumbe and Happy Valley, had been so densely engulfed by foliage that their existence was generally unknown. And the last of the little informal ponds had been reduced to boggy hollows, well on their way to complete disappearance.

This process, so dramatic when set out in print, or when Victorian views of the Commons are compared with their modern equivalents, was rendered less noticeable by its gradual nature. Older residents remembered what the

Tunbridge Wells and Rusthall Commons

Commons had looked like in earlier times, but over the years became accustomed to its new appearance. On the other hand, younger folk, and those recently moved into the area, naturally imagined that this was how the Commons were meant to be. Almost all shared a general perception that 'nature looks after itself', failing to realize that, in England at least, no landscape is entirely natural but must inevitably be the product of a conscious or unconscious collaboration between human activity and natural processes.

The vital stimulus that encouraged many to look at the Commons in a fresh way was the famous Great Storm on the night of 15-16 October 1987. Local people awoke to discover that enormous numbers of trees which had appeared to be permanent features of the landscape had met a premature end. Although not as devastated as some areas, the trees on the Commons had suffered considerable losses. The Commons Conservators now had to consider how the damage could be repaired, and in doing so they were prompted to investigate the original appearance of the Commons, using the Museum's collection of historic views. The Conservators decided to commission the Kent Trust for Nature Conservation to do further research on the history of the Commons, to conduct an environmental survey, and on the basis of these to prepare a detailed management plan. With the help of various experts, both local and from farther afield, an extensive report was prepared for consideration by the Conservators and for public consultation, and its recommendations were formally adopted by the Conservators in 1992. At the same time, public interest in the Commons had considerably increased, resulting in the establishment of the Friends of Tunbridge Wells and Rusthall Commons in 1991.

Since 1992 considerable progress has been made in implementing the new management plan, which does not aim to put the clock back to 1900, but to achieve a mosaic of diverse habitats, of which woodland will still form a part. A number of areas of scrub have been cleared, of which the north west corner of Tunbridge Wells Common is now a particularly attractive example. The surviving patches of heather are being encouraged to spread, the most striking progress being seen in an area beside the Race Course where the plants had almost been shaded out of existence. Grassland areas too are being expanded, and their characteristic butterflies are already increasing and spreading to new areas, assisted by the wider fringes of the footpaths where grasses and flowers have space to flourish. Fir Tree Pond, Bracken Cottage Pond, and the Marl Pits are coming back to life, providing homes for dragonflies, amphibians and other creatures. And lost rock formations at Mount Edgcumbe, Denny Bottom and Happy Valley have been once more exposed to view. Much more remains to be done, but a fine start has been made towards making the Commons as attractive to locals and visitors, and to their native plants and animals, as they were a century ago.

A History and Natural History

Vale Royal, London Road, and Tunbridge Wells Common, *c.*1880.

A similar view, March 2000.

Tunbridge Wells and Rusthall Commons

Rocks at Tunbridge Wells. A watercolour of the St Helena caves and London Road by James Lambert, 1786.

A History and Natural History

The Pantiles viewed from Bath Square, *c.*1860.

A similar view, December 2000.

Tunbridge Wells and Rusthall Commons

Brighton Lake, Eridge Road, *c.*1903. Photograph by J. Welch, with, from left to right, Mrs Jessie and Lilian Kember and Mrs and Dorothy Welch

A similar view, April 2000.

A History and Natural History

HISTORY OF THE MANOR OF RUSTHALL
Roger Farthing

Early History

The Manor of Rusthall originated as part of the Manor of Wrotham which had belonged to the Archbishop of Canterbury since Domesday. There are references to Rusthall in the Custumal of Wrotham of 1283,[1] and Wrotham court rolls of the fifteenth and sixteenth centuries contain scattered references to Rusthall men being fined for not attending the manorial court.[2] In 1531 the Archbishop of Canterbury leased some 'tenements of Rusthall, parcel of Wrotham Manor' to Lord Abergavenny.[3] The earliest references to the Manor of Rusthall as such are in Court Rolls dated 1521 and 1531.[4]

The Weald was an untamed forest mainly used for the feeding of pigs. The northerly parts were settled and belonged to the King or the great Norman lords or to the Church; and each manor then had its own dedicated forest area to the south and its own tracks for the droving of swine to and fro. These pannaging areas were called dens and this is where all the dens in place names come from – Marden, Horsmonden and so on – and it may well be that Bishops Down, which was the old name for Tunbridge Wells Common, is a distant memory of a den belonging to the Archbishop. Over the course of centuries timber became valuable for houses and ships and then for iron smelting, a growing population took over cleared areas for cultivation and dens turned into manors.[5]

Wrotham Manor continued in Canterbury ownership until 1537 when Archbishop Thomas Cranmer gave the manors of Wrotham, Maidstone and others to Henry VIII.[6] Then in 1550 the next King, Edward VI, granted the Manor of Wrotham and other land to Sir John Mason.[7] Sir John sold to Robert Byng between 1556 and 1557[8] and the Byng family in the person of George Byng had the lordship of Rusthall Manor in 1651.[9] A clear line of descent can therefore be traced from the Archbishop to the mid-seventeenth century.

There is however a contradictory story to be found in local sources like the Colbran Guides of the nineteenth century[10] which has its origins in the Kent historians Edward Hasted,[11] John Harris[12] and Thomas Philipott.[13] This tells us that the Manor of Rusthall was sold in the 1400s to Richard Waller of Groombridge who sold it in 1583 to George Stacy who then sold it to Robert Byng whose descendants sold to Richard Constable who sold to Francis Dashwood. Unfortunately the last two stages are quite incorrect and cast doubt on the whole farrago. There is no evidence when and how Rusthall became independent but there is no doubt that the Wrotham-based Byngs relinquished their lordship in about 1660 and the rising importance of the medicinal spring within the Manor boundaries must surely have been a factor.

Tunbridge Wells and Rusthall Commons

The new Lord was Charles Muskerry who in 1664 erected an archway over the 'Wells' bearing his initials and the year.[14] Lord Muskerry had married Margaret de Burgh, heiress to the neighbouring manor of South Frith, whose seat was Somerhill House at Tonbridge; and it may be guessed that this inheritance was supplemented by the purchase of Rusthall Manor. At any rate the 'brave young nobleman' was 'remarkably fond of the place' wrote Benge Burr a century after the events[15] and carried out the work on the spring at his own expense – all in compliment to his royal mistress Queen Katharine who had visited in 1663[16] and whose further visit was expected. Sadly Lord Muskerry was killed in a sea battle with the Dutch in 1665 and the two manors devolved on his widow.

Before his death Lord Muskerry had mortgaged the Manors of Stockhill, Sudmershill and Rusthall with 'all water springs and wells of water thereunto belonging' for £200,[17] but by 16 September 1672 the mortgage had not been redeemed and her ladyship, now Countess Purbeck, let the Manor for seventeen years to Richard Constable at a rent of £18 a year of which £12 was to pay the mortgage interest.[18] Hasted and others unfortunately say that one of the Byngs 'passed the manor away'[19] to Richard Constable who sold it to Sir Francis Dashwood – thus skipping two whole stages in the story of the Manor.

What happened was that Constable agreed to give up his lease when it had seven years more to run; and the three manors were conveyed to Thomas Neale for £228 in 1682.[20] Thomas Neale, the real creator of the Pantiles, was known as 'Golden Neal' as a result of his somewhat unconventional marriage to Lady Gould, which Samuel Pepys records in his diary for 20 June 1664: ' . . . the rich widow, my lady Gould, is married to one Neale, after he had received a box on the eare by her brother . . . '

In 1678 Neale was groom porter to Charles II and Master of the Royal Mint.[21] Four years later he was busying himself with the development of the Pantiles, persuading the freehold tenants of the Manor to accept ten shillings a year as compensation for loss of grazing rights and arranging the building of shops, not lodging houses. By this time Neale's thoughts were turning to a major development project at Seven Dials in London[22] and he sold the Manor in 1689 or 1690 to Thomas Dashwood.

Thomas was the brother of the better known Samuel and Francis Dashwood. They prospered in the silk trade after the Restoration and Samuel became Lord Mayor of London in 1702.[23] Samuel and Francis jointly bought the Manor of Rusthall from their brother for £4100.[24] Samuel died in 1705, then Francis was created baronet in 1707 and sold the Manor in 1720. The Dashwood reign appears to have been uneventful but their successor, Maurice Conyers, an Irishman, also known as O'Connor, was faced with the expiry of fifty year leases running from 1682. This occasioned the protracted lawsuit

A History and Natural History

Thomas Neale Esq. depicted on a medal of 1694.

Pencil sketch of Castle Cottage and Castle Road by J.J. Dodd (1810-94)

Tunbridge Wells and Rusthall Commons

between the lord and his tenants which culminated in the Rusthall Manor Act of 1739. Conyers died intestate between August 1740 and July 1741, leaving as heir his twelve year old eldest son John.[25] On 16 March 1749 John O'Connor, whose address is given as Mount Pleasant, Ireland, attained his majority and a draft deed of 1750 is concerned with the confirmation of his inheritance. Incidentally a list of tenants bundled with this deed says that the premises are 'vastly out of repair' and the rents too high. Perhaps all this dissuaded John O'Connor from preserving his inheritance; the fact is anyway that he soon disposed of it to George Kelley – whose descendants have held it ever since.

Sir George Kelley

George Kelley was probably born in Portsmouth in 1713, the only boy in a family of three elder sisters – Anne, Hannah and Martha. Anne, born in 1708, was married[26] in Portsmouth in 1735 to Thomas Shorey, later an Army Captain guarding the dockyards.[27] George obtained the Licentiate of the College of Physicians and an Aberdeen MD in 1743, but he must have been frequenting the medical honeypot of Tunbridge Wells some time before this since in October 1743 he married[28] a local woman, Johanna Cock, who owned a house on Bishops Down, roughly where the Spa Hotel now stands[29] – but there appear to have been no children of the marriage.

Kelley's name appears in the vestry minutes of the Chapel of King Charles the Martyr several times from 1748 onwards, and in 1754 he and the recently widowed Duchess of Bolton (the former actress and creator of the role of Polly Peachum) appear together as donors of one half and one guinea respectively. About this time Kelley seems to have come into money and began buying up properties on Bishops Down so that within a few years he had spent £6,600 on eighteen purchases and he capped this with the purchase of the Manor of Rusthall for £12,000 in 1758.[30] During this time he is said to have cured the Dowager Duchess of a painful illness[31] and when she died in 1760 she made him her executor and residuary legatee[32] in which role he had to supervise the installation in the chapel roof of a 'new best 8-day clock' for which the Duchess bequeathed £66 and which we call Polly Peachum's to this day in her memory.[33]

Kelley became a JP and then in 1761 he was appointed Sheriff of Kent. At the conclusion of his year of office, in September 1762, he was knighted.[34] He now turned his attention to the construction of a mansion house befitting his station. The result was the building on the site of his wife's house which with later additions now houses the Spa Hotel. Certain rainwater hopper heads embossed 'GK 1764' attest the date.

In 1766 Benge Burr published his history of Tunbridge Wells and manages

A History and Natural History

to say one thing about Kelley: 'These [horse races] are principally supported by the present lord of the manor, Sir George Kelley, who frequently, since he came to the estate, has given a silver cup for this purpose'.[35] Another institution, revived by Kelley, was that of manorial courts. He held a court on 11 October in the year of his purchase, 1758, and tidied up the affairs of the previous twenty-eight years; and six more courts thereafter.

Sometime before his death Sir George composed a memorandum book[36] containing particulars of his estate. It was addressed to his brother-in-law, James Spagg, a surgeon of Limehouse, Middlesex,[37] who was one of his executors. It reveals that Kelley owned Hollands Manor (at Langton Green) as well as Rusthall, gives advice about the management of farms and tenants, the annual payment of rents at his house on 24 August, the whereabouts of keys and 'writings' including the Manor Court Books, the holding of courts leet and baron, the division of gratuities among the 'dippers',[38] the avoidance of lawsuits and how to get on with Lady Kelley and the neighbours and 'the people of the Wells'. 'Let me from long experience advise my relations and executors to avoid any law suits especially with my wife Lady Kelley least they repent it to their cost and when it is too late . . . Be civill to all the Wells people but in general they are very artful and designing. Therefore be very cautious and keep yourselves very much to yourselves but be moderately hospitable and sociable with a few country neighbours.'

Sir George wrote his will on 4 July 1771[39] and died in November at the rather young age of fifty-eight. He left his wife Johanna £100 but no life interest in the Manor and estate which went to his three sisters equally. He left £50 and all his books and bookcases to James Spagg; and £50 to his nephew Samuel Gardner, the two latter to be his executors. A codicil made a fortnight later gives an annuity of £50 to a certain Mrs Ann Lishon of Charlotte Street, Bloomsbury – whose connection with Sir George remains a mystery. The Speldhurst Register shows that he was buried on 19 November and a 1939 churchyard survey[40] reported an inscription saying he died on 10 November.

The Kelley Descendants

For eight years after Sir George's death, his three sisters reigned jointly as Ladies of the Manor. Then Hannah Tanner died in 1780[41] and Martha Spagg and Anne Shorey continued their joint ladyship until 1796 when they died within six months of each other.[42] The sisters did not however take over Sir George's mansion house. It was sold in 1772 to Martin Yorke Esq.,[43] a retired East India Company major – from whom of course we now have Major York's Road – and the house, known as Bishops Down Grove, continued in separate ownership from the Manor. The Ladies of the Manor, then and later, with

Tunbridge Wells and Rusthall Commons

The Bath House, the Pantiles. Engraved by Letitia Byrne after a drawing by Paul Amsinck, 1810

Diana Menuhin and Griselda Kentner attend the Tunbridge Wells 350th anniversary celebrations at the Pantiles, September 1956

The Honourable Jeremy Menuhin

A History and Natural History

their relatives, occupied, or used as lodging houses for letting, the smaller houses on the strip of land to the east of the big house which Sir George had bought about the same time as the Manor.

One thing that Sir George Kelley and those who came after him were not good at was producing descendants. The story of the next two centuries is one of nephews and nieces and descent through the female line, as is illustrated in the family tree. Take the Kelley siblings. George and Johanna were childless, Hannah married to Tanner certainly had no surviving children and died in 1780; and similarly Martha Spagg who died in 1796; only Anne who married Thomas Shorey in 1735 had three daughters but she died in the same year as Martha leaving her daughters next in line of succession.

Of Anne Shorey's three daughters however Ann had died in 1775 at the age of thirty-five.[44] Her husband Samuel Gardner (one of Kelley's executors) had died shortly before and their orphaned children were left in the guardianship of Anne's sister Elizabeth.[45] Another daughter, Mary, married to Captain Henry Lloyd RN, was still living in 1796 and could in theory have inherited the Manor either alone or jointly, but Anne Shorey's will,[46] made in 1785, had given Mary property in Langton Green and Rotherfield and the house she and her husband were living in with other property on Bishops Down but left the Manor and residue of the estate to the unmarried Elizabeth. In fact Mary died before 1799, already a widow, and left her property to her sister;[47] but her house continued to be known as 'Lloyds House' for many years. So in 1796 Miss (usually 'Mrs' honorifically) Elizabeth Shorey became sole Lady of the Manor; and we should not forget that it was she who in 1804 built the Bath House over the Pantiles spring.

The succession devolved next on Elizabeth's wards, the children of her sister Ann Gardner[48] who had died back in 1775. These were George, Elizabeth, Thomas Christopher and Rosamund. The eldest son, George, died however in January 1790 at the age of twenty-two and was joined in November by his twenty-one year old sister Elizabeth.[49] Therefore when Miss Shorey died in March 1823 the second son, Thomas Christopher Gardner, inherited. She was eighty-seven years old, according to a newspaper report:[50] 'The remains of Mrs Shorey, Lady of the Manor of Rusthall . . . were deposited in the family vault at Speldhurst on Sunday, the 30th ult . . . A considerable and respectable body of tenantry, principally inhabitants of the Wells, headed the procession, followed by two mourning coaches and private carriages; the concourse of spectators was very great.'

Thomas Christopher Gardner's lordship of the Manor lasted until 1839; but he was a somewhat footloose character. In 1796 his address was 'late of Bishops Down, now of St Albans Street, Pall Mall'. But he then became a soldier because, according to Amsinck,[51] writing in 1810, he was 'late major,

Tunbridge Wells and Rusthall Commons

95th Regiment of Foot, served with credit in Holland, Egypt and South America'. A document[52] among the Manor papers dated 10 August 1825 next reveals that his sister Rosamund had over a period lent him £3099 6s. 0d. and agreed to take a number of houses and fields in discharge of the debt. Rosamund was married to Francis Weller, 'late Lieutenant Colonel in the 13th Regiment of Foot but now of Rusthall'. The document was witnessed by two of their sons, Francis, Lieutenant Royal Artillery, and, most interestingly, Thomas M.M. (the future 'Colonel Weller') who signed as 'Clerk to Mr Scoones', the Tonbridge solicitor.

Major Gardner does not seem to have been at home in his Manor. He went to live in Namur in Belgium and on 16 June 1832 gave a comprehensive power of attorney[53] to William and John Scoones. The next sight of him is on 1 January 1840[54] when he conveyed the manors of Rusthall, Stockhill and Sudmershill, some land and houses and his share of the Walks Estate to Francis Weller of Woolwich, Captain Royal Artillery. It would appear from documents[55] which came to light very recently and have not been closely examined that the Major was to receive an annuity of £6000 in return for the early release of the estate which would have come to Capt. Weller by inheritance in due course. He died at Clifton, Gloucestershire, three years later and administration was granted on 28 September 1843 to his widow Sarah Elizabeth. There do not appear to have been any children of the marriage but the Manor inheritance had already merged, by the conveyance of 1840 and through sister Rosamund's marriage, with that of the Wellers of Kingsgate House, Rolvenden.

The Weller Estate

The Weller family was founded by Alexander Weller in the sixteenth century.[56] They were wealthy clothiers of Cranbrook who bought land in Sussex, in Essex and at Tonbridge in Kent. One branch married into the Poley family of Boxted, Suffolk, and took the name Weller-Poley. The other branch had the Kingsgate Estate with its mansion house at Rolvenden, not far from Cranbrook. This estate was held in 1828 by Robert Weller[57] who was unmarried, and the estate descended to his nephews, the sons of Francis and Rosamund – and the same sons were heirs through their mother to the Rusthall Manor estate.

Rosamund's husband Francis was the great-great-great-grandson of Alexander Weller of Kingsgate House who died in 1671.[58] Francis was one of five sons and two daughters of Nicholas who in 1750 married Catharine, daughter of Bishop Carr of Killaloe in Ireland. Three of these sons were in the army; two died unmarried in the East Indies and the third, also unmarried, died in 1791 and is buried at Rolvenden. That left Robert and Francis; and since Robert was childless, his nephews succeeded in turn. There were three boys and one girl. The eldest nephew William, a midshipman in the navy, died unmarried 'on the coast of Africa' in 1824 and therefore the second, another Francis, came into the combined estates of Kingsgate and Rusthall; but the third nephew, Thomas Montagu Martin, and the niece, Rosamund Mary Anne, both had their part to play.

Francis Weller might be called the invisible Lord of Rusthall Manor. None of the local books so much as mention him, conflating him perhaps with the brother who came next. But he did hold two Courts Baron, one in 1841 and another in 1847 when 'Rules for the Dippers' were formulated; and his name appears as owner of all the Manor properties in the Tithe Map and Award of *c.*1840. By 1849 he had gone to live with his sister, Rosamund Mary Ann, married to Alfred Suart, Rector of Waldringfield, Suffolk; where he died in 1853, leaving everything to his brother, Thomas Montagu Martin Weller, except an annuity to his sister and £1000 in trust for her daughter, Emma Rosamund Mary. His library and (mentioned for the first time) family pictures went to his brother.[59]

If Francis was the invisible Lord of the Manor, his brother Thomas Montagu Martin Weller held sway for over thirty years, leaving however a somewhat enigmatic impression. He was a Weller and very proud of the family name – and yet he married two Scottish ladies and never produced an heir. He was always known as Colonel Weller and yet he was only a part-time lieutenant colonel in the West Kent Light Infantry Regiment of Militia; and he was a JP but started life as apprentice in a solicitor's office. He was born in December 1803 and married first in 1834 – in Glasgow.[60] His bride was Christian Jane, daughter of John Baird Esq. JP, manager of the Shotts Iron Works, Lanarkshire.

In 1839 Thomas Montagu inherited the Kingsgate estate from his uncle Robert Weller and in 1853, when his brother Francis died, he took over the reins of Rusthall Manor and was to hold them for thirty-five years. In 1865 he renewed the basins at the spring,[61] but he appears to have been more at home at the Weller residence in Rolvenden than in his Manor. In 1866 his wife died and three years later, in an episode of unexpected romanticism, he married at the British Embassy in Paris[62] the widow of Dr James Frederick Steuart of the Bengal Cavalry – who was also the sister-in-law of the late Mrs Weller's brother. The new Mrs Weller, born Mary Anne Sword, had been married no more than two years to Dr Frederick Steuart when he died in India in 1846; and one child, a daughter Constance, had been born. When mother remarried therefore Constance must have been in her twenties and she came and lived with her mother and stepfather at Kingsgate House.

Col. Weller died on 15 April 1888 in his eighty-fifth year at Kingsgate 'where he had resided for many years'[63] and Kingsgate House is the address he gives in his will[64] which reveals a considerable pride in the Weller name –

so much so that he desires anyone marrying a Weller who may inherit the estate and the family heirlooms to 'take and use upon all occasions the surname of Weller either in addition to or in substitution' for his own and to bear the arms of Weller. All his landed property he leaves to two trustees for the benefit of his wife during her life; then to his niece, Emma Rosamund Mary Suart, for her life; then to her sons, if any, followed by her daughters, if any; then, all else failing, to the sons, in order of seniority, of his first wife's brother, Adam Baird; and finally to his own 'right heirs' for ever. He then provides for the family heirlooms. These consist of a library of books and their bookcases, the family portraits and other pictures in Kingsgate House and all the silver plate. Two copies of an inventory of the heirlooms are to be signed by the trustees and by each successive owner who is to insure house and heirlooms adequately.

After the Colonel

The upshot of Col. Weller's will was initially that his widow, Mary Anne, backed by the two trustees F.O. Baird and R.W. Tweedie, became Lady of the Manor until her death in 1899. The great event of this period was the case of the gents' convenience. The town council built this under part of the Upper Walk of the Pantiles. The dispute reached the House of Lords in 1896, the Manor, in the person mainly of F.O. Baird, objecting. The outcome, according to the local press at the time,[65] was that, in return for her costs of about £2000 and another large cost to the town, she had 'simply obtained a barren declaration of her right to the soil of the Pantiles'. When Mrs Weller died the Manor came briefly to Emma Rosamund Mary Suart, the daughter of Rosamund and the Revd Alfred Suart; but she had never married and the succession passed therefore, on her death in 1904 to the trustee Frank Osborne, the only surviving son of Adam Baird, brother of the first Mrs Weller.

Rosamund Suart did however leave behind a lengthy will which, among much else, specified the family portraits already mentioned: Sir Charles Meredith, Bishop Carr, Sir George Kelley and Mrs Gardner by Angelica Kaufmann, Mrs Weller, Captain Francis Weller, Mrs Shorey, and 'my mother Mrs Suart née Weller'. Bishop Carr figures in Berry's Genealogy as the maternal grandfather of Col. Francis Weller; but the attribution to Angelica Kaufmann must be treated with caution.[66]

Baird was a reclusive bachelor who for twenty-five years never left his house in Hove. This did not prevent him from taking a keen interest in the affairs of the Manor. He 'scanned the local press every week to see if any Manorial Tenants had died, writing to mention this to the Agents so that . . . they could pursue the matter of a Heriot [the best beast due to the lord on the death of a tenant] . . . . In one exchange he was seriously contemplating claiming

A History and Natural History

Royal Victoria Grove, *c.*1912.

A similar view, October 2000.

Tunbridge Wells and Rusthall Commons

The Pantiles, Tunbridge Wells. Thomas Loggan's gouache painting of the northern end of the Pantiles showing the enclosure and archway erected by Charles Muskerry, *c.*1740

Watercolour of George Kelley's house at Bishops Down, late eighteenth-century

A History and Natural History

Manor portraits. Both appear to be those attributed to Angelica Kaufmann by Rosamund Suart. They may be George Kelley and Ann Gardner.

The Parson's Nose Rock. A watercolour by Charles Tattershall Dodd, *c.*1840

Tunbridge Wells and Rusthall Commons

Denny Bottom and the Loaf Rock, *c.*1880

A similar view, March 2000.

A History and Natural History

a fox terrier, and only desisted when the dead Tenant's housekeeper insisted that the animal was hers, not her master's.'[67]

Under the terms of Col. Weller's will, if F.O. Baird had no children the succession terminated with the colonel's 'right heirs' and extensive searches were therefore carried out to discover whether in earlier life Baird had married or had children – but nothing was found. Col. Weller's 'right heir' meant the senior male representative of the Suart family who at the beginning was Miss Emma Rosamund Mary Suart's cousin, General William Hodgson Suart. Baird was known as the 'life tenant' and was envisaged as a stop gap until the General could take over. The Suart family had come into the picture because of Rosamund Weller's marriage in 1846 to Alfred Suart, whose father Edward seems to have moved to Tunbridge Wells from Lancaster and sent his son to Tonbridge School from 1829 to 1835. He was spotted with 'A. Suart Esq.' among the company dining in honour of Princess Victoria's birthday at the Royal Victoria and Sussex Hotel – and we can imagine that it was at some such social gathering in Tunbridge Wells that young Alfred Suart met his future wife, Rosamund Weller. Alfred went up to Sidney Sussex College, Cambridge, and joined the Church in 1843, becoming Rector of Waldringfield in 1846. In 1862 he retired to live in Brighton and then at Lloyds House on Bishops Down.

In the event General Suart died unexpectedly in 1923 and the 'stop gap' Baird lived to be ninety-five. In 1949 therefore it was General Suart's only child, Daisy Evelyn, a pianist of some note, who became Lady of the Manor; she however enjoyed her position for a few months only and in 1950 the succession passed jointly to her husband and her two daughters by her first marriage to Gerard Louis Gould who had died at thirty.[68] In 1951 the Tunbridge Wells Advertiser wrote in its Festival of Britain booklet: 'The present Lord and Ladies of the Manor are perhaps the most colourful in its long history. . . . Admiral Sir Cecil Harcourt is Commander-in-Chief the Nore and his stepdaughters are the wives of two of the best known figures in the world of music. Mrs Diana Menuhin became the wife of violinist Yehudi Menuhin in 1947 and Mrs Griselda Kentner was married to pianist Louis Kentner in 1946'.[69] The Admiral having died in 1959 and Lady Menuhin, owing to pressure of other activities, having resigned her title, Mrs Kentner shared the honour with her nephews, Jeremy and Gerard Menuhin, until her death in 1996 when the title devolved on the Honourable Jeremy Menuhin, the concert pianist.

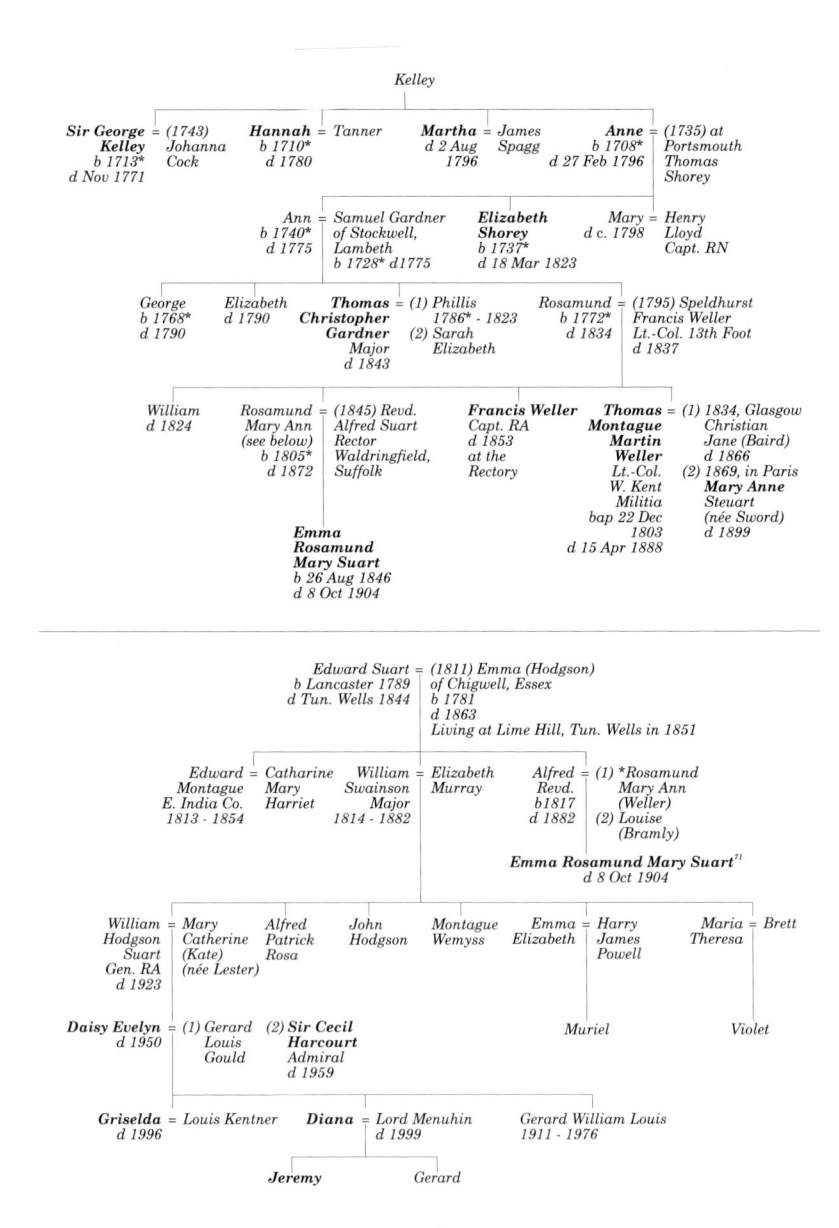

Tunbridge Wells and Rusthall Commons

Kelley

Sir George Kelley b 1713* d Nov 1771 = (1743) **Hannah** b 1710* d 1780 Johanna Cock

Hannah = Tanner

Martha = James Spagg, d 2 Aug 1796

Anne b 1708* d 27 Feb 1796 = (1735) at Portsmouth Thomas Shorey

Ann b 1740* d 1775 = Samuel Gardner of Stockwell, Lambeth b 1728* d 1775

Elizabeth Shorey b 1737* d 18 Mar 1823

Mary d c. 1798 = Henry Lloyd Capt. RN

George b 1768* d 1790

Elizabeth d 1790

Thomas Christopher Gardner Major d 1843 = (1) Phillis 1786* - 1823 (2) Sarah Elizabeth

Rosamund b 1772* d 1834 = (1795) Speldhurst Francis Weller Lt.-Col. 13th Foot d 1837

William d 1824

Rosamund Mary Ann (see below) b 1805* d 1872 = (1845) Revd. Alfred Suart Rector Waldringfield, Suffolk

Emma Rosamund Mary Suart b 26 Aug 1846 d 8 Oct 1904

Francis Weller Capt. RA d 1853 at the Rectory

Thomas Montague Martin Weller Lt.-Col. W. Kent Militia bap 22 Dec 1803 d 15 Apr 1888 = (1) 1834, Glasgow Christian Jane (Baird) d 1866 (2) 1869, in Paris **Mary Anne** Steuart (née Sword) d 1899

Edward Suart b Lancaster 1789 d Tun. Wells 1844 = (1811) Emma (Hodgson) of Chigwell, Essex b 1781 d 1863
Living at Lime Hill, Tun. Wells in 1851

Edward Montague E. India Co. 1813 - 1854 = Catharine Mary Harriet

William Swainson Major 1814 - 1882 = Elizabeth Murray

Alfred Revd. b1817 d 1882 = (1) *Rosamund Mary Ann (Weller) (2) Louise (Bramly)

Emma Rosamund Mary Suart[71] d 8 Oct 1904

William Hodgson Suart Gen. RA d 1923 = Mary Catherine (Kate) (née Lester)

Alfred Patrick Rosa

John Hodgson

Montague Wemyss

Emma Elizabeth = Harry James Powell

Maria Theresa = Brett

Daisy Evelyn d 1950 = (1) Gerard Louis Gould (2) **Sir Cecil Harcourt** Admiral d 1959

Muriel

Violet

Griselda d 1996 = Louis Kentner

Diana = Lord Menuhin d 1999

Gerard William Louis 1911 - 1976

Jeremy

Gerard

Pedigree – Sir George Kelley to the Present Day[70]

A History and Natural History

NOTES

[1] Canterbury Cathedral Archives, E24 f76v and 79 (private communication Jayne Semple).
[2] Centre for Kentish Studies (CKS) U55 M13, M14, M21 and M22 (Jayne Semple).
[3] Kent Archaeological Society (KAS) Records publication vol XVIII p. 295, 6 Mar 1531.
[4] Lambeth Palace, Archiepiscopal estates, Court Rolls ED342 and CKS U1475 M16. For comment and background reading see Jellis 1985, Chap 1 pp. 2-4 in particular.
[5] Witney 1976 passim.
[6] Lambeth Palace, CM XII/23, 30 Nov 1537.
[7] *Calendar of Patent Rolls,* Edward VI Vol III p. 197, 4 May 1550.
[8] CKS U55 M20 Wrotham Manor court rolls 1 Oct 1556/10 May 1557 (Jayne Semple).
[9] CKS U749 M1, 2 and 3. An analysis of the 12 courts held between 1651 and 1694 faces p. 20 in Jellis 1985.
[10] Phippen 1844, pp. 100-101.
[11] Hasted 1797, vol III p. 283.
[12] Harris 1719, p. 293.
[13] Philipott 1776, pp. 320-21.
[14] British Museum Add MSS 5233 f52, reproduced in Farthing 1990 plate 10 and Hembrey 1990 plate IV.
[15] Burr 1766, pp. 40-44.
[16] For a discussion of the dates of this and other royal visits to the Wells see Farthing 1990, Notes and References pp. 4-11.
[17] CKS U749 E25.
[18] Ibid.
[19] See note 11 above.
[20] CKS U749 E25.
[21] *Dictionary of National Biography.*
[22] See appeal document, The Seven Dials Monument Company, 1 Shorts Gardens, Seven Dials, London WC2H 9AT.
[23] Dashwood 1987, pp. 12-17.
[24] Buckinghamshire Record Office D/D/18/24.
[25] CKS U749 E29.
[26] Portsmouth City Museums and Records Services, personal communication 5 May 1999
[27] A large collection of Manor papers was transferred from the offices of Ibbett Mosely, Manor agents, to CKS in 1999 after provisional cataloguing by Brenda and Geoffrey Copus and the author. The CKS reference is U749

Tunbridge Wells and Rusthall Commons

Additional which will be used with a provisional catalogue reference where relevant. Among the collection was found the original commission, signed by Henry Fox, of Shorey as Captain of the Guard at Portsmouth Dockyard in 1755 (Farthing 203, Bundle 1 No 46).

[28] CKS U785 T2
[29] John Bowra's 1738 map can be found at Farthing 1990, plate 47
[30] CKS U749 E32, and particularly E35, which includes a notebook containing 'A Particular of my estate in the County of Kent and elsewhere, and of whom bought and what was ye purchase money'.
[31] Hamilton 1905 pp. 2-3.
[32] CKS U749 E31.
[33] CKS U749 Q1 records some of the problems of installation.
[34] Shaw vol II has: '1762 Sept 29 George Kelley of Bishopsdown, Speldhurst, Kent, and Sheriff of that county'.
[35] Burr 1766 pp. 125-26.
[36] CKS U749 E35.
[37] See Spagg's will at CKS U785 T4.
[38] For more on a dispute among the 'dippers' in 1768, see 'The Dippers' Tale' in *Common Ground*, Newsletter of the Friends of Tunbridge Wells and Rusthall Commons, December 1995.
[39] CKS U749 T2.
[40] Personal communication, Guy Hitchings, archivist, Speldhurst.
[41] 1 April 1780 according to records of gravestone inscriptions, personal communication, Guy Hitchings, archivist, Speldhurst.
[42] Anne Shorey died 27 February 1796, CKS P344/1/5 (Speldhurst Burials). Martha Spagg does not appear, but she died 2 August 1796 according to some private papers of Mrs Kentner.
[43] Sprange 1786, p. 88.
[44] See note 41 above.
[45] CKS U749 T35.
[46] CKS U785 T4.
[47] CKS U785 T2.
[48] See note 45 above.
[49] See note 41 above.
[50] *Maidstone Journal* 8 April 1823.
[51] Amsinck 1810, p. 18.
[52] CKS U785 T2.
[53] CKS U785 T26.
[54] CKS U749 L2 Bundle 5.
[55] CKS U749 Additional.
[56] According to some private papers of Mrs Kentner.

A History and Natural History

[57] See Berry 1830, pp. 46-7.
[58] Berry loc cit.
[59] Will proved London 21 February 1853.
[60] A copy of the marriage certificate (St George's Parish, Glasgow, February 1834) is in CKS U749 Additional (Copus L 68).
[61] Savidge 1975, p. 136.
[62] The embassy certificate is in CKS U749 Additional (Farthing 207).
[63] *Kent and Sussex Courier* April 1888.
[64] Proved London 4 October 1888.
[65] *Tunbridge Wells Advertiser* 21 August 1896.
[66] Most unfortunately the portraits have all been either mislaid or cannot be identified. Two paintings were hanging in the dining room at Mrs Kentner's house during her occupancy which may well be the pair attributed to Angelica Kaufmann – George Kelley and Mrs Ann Gardner. Efforts should be made to find and identify any that remain with the family.
[67] CKS U749 Additional, Geoffrey Copus, catalogue introduction.
[68] See Menuhin 1984, p. 8.
[69] *Tunbridge Wells Advertiser,* 'The Manor of Rusthall', but the earlier parts of this account should be checked against evidence.
[70] Dates of birth of Kelley, his sisters, and some other family members (those marked with an asterisk) are calculated from ages at death on Speldhurst tombstone inscriptions which are now illegible but were recorded some years ago. See note 41 above.
[71] Emma Rosamund Mary Suart was succeeded until 1949 by the life tenant Frank Osborne Baird.

Tunbridge Wells and Rusthall Commons

GEOLOGY AND PALAEONTOLOGY
Ed Jarzembowski

Introduction.
'Tunbridge Wells is situated on and has given its name to one of the fresh water strata forming the central Weald' wrote J.C.M. Given in *Royal Tunbridge Wells: Past and Present* (1946). He continued 'Thus it is incumbent on us to consider how this corner of southeast England has assumed its present curious form.' The answer lies in the geology which is discussed in this essay.

The Wealden of the Weald.
The central Weald is a largely flat, heavy clay country in its outer part, while the inner portion consists mainly of hills and valleys, supporting a diverse vegetation of contrasting ecology. This difference in landscape and cover reflects the underlying geological layers (strata). The outer part is mainly on mudstones of the Weald Clay deposited during the Hauterivian and Barremian stages of the Early Cretaceous epoch, some 125-135 million years ago (Harland and others 1990). The inner portion is on older sandstones and mudstones of the Hastings beds in turn underlain by limestones and mudstones of the Purbeck beds. These strata were deposited during the Cretaceous Berriasian and Valanginian stages, 135-145 million years ago.

The Hastings beds and Weald Clay together comprise the Wealden beds which are now formally referred to as the Wealden Supergroup. The Wealden beds are typically developed in southern England, especially in the southern part of Kent and adjoining parts of Surrey and Sussex. The Hastings beds (or Group) are also referred to as the Lower Wealden and the Weald Clay formations as the Upper Wealden. The former characterize the High Weald and the latter the Low Weald as explained above. There is only a limited exposure (outcrop) of Purbeck beds (Purbeck Limestone Group) in the central Weald, over the border in East Sussex.

The Hastings beds are divided into five major sandstone and mudstone divisions (Bristow and Bazley 1972). These divisions or formations are named after various localities where the rocks were observed by early geologists. The Tunbridge Wells Sand lies in the upper part of the group and extends widely across the Weald away from the town itself. The Tunbridge Wells Sand is commonly split into two formations (Upper and Lower Tunbridge Wells Sand) by the intervening Grinstead Clay Formation which is especially well developed in the western Weald. The Lower Tunbridge Wells Sand is underlain by the Wadhurst Clay Formation which, in turn, rests on the Ashdown Formation.

A History and Natural History

Geological structure.
Examination of a geological map (Gallois and Edmunds 1965, plate 1) of south-east England shows that the Weald Clay has an outcrop resembling a skewed horseshoe arching to the west, with the open end on the English Channel. Cretaceous post-Wealden strata such as the Gault, Greensand and Chalk show a similar outcrop with oppositely curved northern and southern limbs or narrow belts. These Cretaceous rocks dip under Lower Tertiary (Palaeogene) strata to the north and south of the central Weald, and the same structure continues under the English Channel into northern France.

What we now see is essentially an eroded, faulted upfold or anticline on a roughly east-west axis with a westerly plunge towards Hampshire. This major anticline and associated minor folds was produced by the shortening of the earth's crust in southern England during the Alpine mountain-building phase (orogeny) when Italy collided with Europe. This movement was not sudden but was spread over a long interval of geological time, probably reaching a maximum in late Tertiary times, some twenty or more million years ago. Prolonged erosion has removed the top of this oval dome. Royal Tunbridge Wells is located on the northern limb of the Wealden anticline, not too far from the main axis, where some of the oldest rocks in southern England have been pushed up to the surface.

Wealden soils and springs.
The Wealden rocks weather to produce acidic, relatively infertile and poorly drained soils of stagnogley or stagnogley-with-brown-earth types. The former differs by being more clayey and its texture has been described as 'like soup in winter and cement in summer' whilst the latter has been called a 'sportsman's paradise and a farmer's hell' due to a combination of steep slopes and poor soils (McRae and Burnham 1976). The alternation of porous sand and impervious clayey strata gives rise to a number of streams including the well-publicized, iron-rich chalybeate springs of Royal Tunbridge Wells which issue from the lower part of the Tunbridge Wells Sand.

Origin of the Wealden.
The Wealden beds, especially the sandy parts of the Hastings beds, have been studied extensively for the past half century by Professor Perce Allen F.R.S. at the University of Reading. Through his work (see Allen 1990 and references therein) we can now explain these alternating sandstone and mudstone formations as representing repeat phases of river and wetland development in south-east England during Early Cretaceous times. In our area, the river/s flowed mainly from the north where an upland area existed on the site of the present-day Thames valley. From transported pebbles in the Wealden, e.g.

Tunbridge Wells and Rusthall Commons

Tunbridge Wells Common, we know that the uplands were of Jurassic and older rocks. Over the millennia, the rivers eroded the upland depositing sediment in the Weald which was turned into a gently subsiding basin. Eventually, the uplands were so eroded that the rivers became sluggish and mud instead of sand accumulated in the basin. Earth movements along faults at the edge of the basin then rejuvenated the uplands and the cycle started again. In the basin, a pile of sand, silt and clay about a kilometre thick accumulated forming the basis of the modern Wealden beds. The Early Cretaceous crustal activity in south-east England was probably associated with the initial opening of the North Atlantic Ocean at this time when sea floor spreading occurred just to the west of Ireland. Basin downfaulting ceased after the Hastings beds were deposited as the ocean widened. The south-east disappeared under the sea after Weald Clay times, not to emerge again until the Tertiary.

Wealden climate.

In early Cretaceous times the climate of the Weald was much warmer than today resembling that of the modern Mediterranean (Allen 1998). Conditions were drier in Purbeck times so that salt pans developed as in some Middle East countries today. These evaporite deposits can be extensive and Purbeck gypsum is mined commercially near Mountfield. The climate became more humid in Wealden times and the warm but variable regime included drier episodes e.g. fossil charcoal (fusain) provides evidence of wildfires breaking out.

Wealden fossils.

The Early Cretaceous fauna and flora of the Weald was diverse and quite different in many respects from that of the present day. The fossil evidence ranges from microscopic pollen grains through to large vertebrate skeletal remains. The most famous animals are the dinosaurs and include brontosaur-like sauropods, armoured dinosaurs, and bipedal carnivores and herbivores, the latter known from Withyham and Southborough (Knipe 1916). The carnivores are most popular but rather rare as one might expect, whereas the herbivore *Iguanodon* is probably the commonest Wealden dinosaur. These large reptiles are known not only from bones but also indirect evidence such as stomach stones and footprints, the latter from Crowborough. Other reptiles include flying pterosaurs, swimming turtles, and crocodiles such as *Goniopholis*, also from Southborough. Recently, small reptiles and amphibians have been found in the Weald Clay. Other vertebrates comprise rare small mammals and cartilaginous and bony fish which are relatively common, e.g. hybodont sharks and the thick-scaled shellfish-feeding *Lepidotes*.

A History and Natural History

Reconstruction drawing of an *Iguanodon*

Tunbridge Wells and Rusthall Commons

The vegetation of the Wealden differed markedly from the present day in the scarcity of flowering plants (angiosperms) and lack of grasses. Other seed plants (gymnosperms) were, however, represented by various conifers and a few cycads, cycad-like bennettitaleans, and extinct seed ferns. True ferns (including tree ferns) and horsetails (land and aquatic) were comparatively common and there is even evidence of mosses and liverworts, quillworts, fungi and algae.

Invertebrates are represented by single-cell animals (Foraminifera), snails and mussels (molluscs), worms, various arthropods and even reworked (recycled) fossils. The latter include rare Jurassic ammonites eroded by rivers from the Londinian uplands. The tiny shells of Foraminifera are also rare like other animals which live mainly in salt water e.g. sea urchins. Worms are represented by natural casts of their burrowing activity and microscopic remains of the egg stage. The most common snail is *Viviparus*, a gill-breathing fresh water mollusc the descendants of which are still found living in southeast England today. The extinct mussels *Neomiodon* and *Filosina*, found in the Lower and Upper Wealden respectively, may occur in large numbers and were probably adapted for life in brackish water. Distinct limy beds with massed shells of *Viviparus* and *Neomiodon/Filosina* are referred to as Paludina and Cyrena limestones. These may have colourful local names e.g. Bethersden Marble. Fresh water mussels belonging to the living genus *Unio* are also found, e.g. in the Tunbridge Wells Sand. Arthropods are diverse including seed shrimps (ostracods), clam shrimps (conchostracans), slaters (isopods), a crayfish (decapod) and many insects.

The discovery of these fossil insects prompted a separate chapter by the late Dr Roy Crowson in Given's *Royal Tunbridge Wells*. Many of the fossils were from the Wadhurst Clay of Quarry Hill Brickworks, Tonbridge, which now lies beneath a new housing estate although scheduled as a Site of Special Scientific Interest under a 1947 Act of Parliament. Fortunately, more insects have been found elsewhere in the Wealden and to-date include dragonflies and damselflies (Odonata*), a stonefly (Plecoptera), cockroaches (Blattodea*), a termite (Isoptera), grasshoppers and crickets (Orthoptera*), bugs (Hemiptera*), lacewings (Neuroptera*), snake flies (Raphidioptera), beetles (Coleoptera*), scorpion flies (Mecoptera*), flies (Diptera*), caddisflies (Trichoptera) and sawflies and wasps (Hymenoptera*). Those orders marked above with an asterisk are known from Quarry Hill. Beetle wingcases have also been found at Langton Green, near Royal Tunbridge Wells, in the Lower Tunbridge Wells Sand (Jarzembowski 1987). Borings in wood resembling the activity of larval bark beetles have been described from the Lower Wealden of Crowborough (Jarzembowski 1990). Much work remains to be done on Wealden fossils and new discoveries can be expected.

A History and Natural History

Wealden landforms.
In some places the Wealden sandstones form bare, rounded cliffs especially in the Ardingly Sandstone Member, a subdivision of the Lower Tunbridge Wells Sand. The cliffs have developed due to the relative strength and resistance to erosion of the sandstone compared to strata that lie above and below it (although they are still liable to crumble, e.g. if climbed). Opinion is divided over the exact mode of origin of the cliffs. They are considered to have formed by weathering and downhill movement of detached rock under arctic conditions during the last ice age or under a milder, temperate climate. For various ideas and processes, see Robinson and Williams (1984). In any case, these Quaternary landforms developed during the last few thousand or tens of thousands of years and are relatively young compared to the great antiquity of the rock itself. The Cretaceous sandstone was originally brought up to the surface by earth movements in Tertiary times which are discussed above. The Quaternary cliffs and associated upstanding rocks were once thought to be of coastal origin, a view which is now long rejected. The upstanding rocks may be narrow at the base, forming pedestals, and include famous local landmarks with individual names.

The tallest cliffs, which reach fifteen metres in height, are found at High Rocks near Royal Tunbridge Wells between two small tributaries of the River Medway. The vertical cliff faces are fissured by natural vertical cracks (joints) which are widened and divide the sandstone into a series of isolated blocks. The cliffs are typically undercut towards their base and the whitish or buff yellow sandstone often has a reddish-brown or black crust. There is also honeycomb and tortoiseshell weathering to be seen. In the former, the surface of the sandstone is pitted by numerous small circular hollows, and in the latter the surface is dissected by a polygonal network of cracks.

On Rusthall Common there is an isolated and naturally sculpted sandstone block which is said to resemble a large toad squatting on a pedestal. Nearby, the upper surface of the Ardingly Sandstone is exposed and relatively flat forming a sandstone pavement which is criss-crossed by small joints with some large weathering pits (dish-like hollows). There are also other upstanding rocks besides Toad Rock including the Loaf Rock, the Parson's Nose and the Lion. Such rocks could have become naturally separated from the cliffs by weathering and erosion along vertical joints but some of the surrounding stone might also have been removed by past quarrying activity. The undercutting from all sides and shape of the blocks are, however, natural.

There are other sandstone cliffs in the neighbourhood including at Happy Valley, Tunbridge Wells Common, Chiddinglye Wood, Harrison Rocks (Groombridge), Bowles Rocks, Stones Farm (Saint Hill), Wakehurst Place (Ardingly), Sheffield Forest, Eridge Rocks, and Penn's Rocks. Fresh sandstone

Tunbridge Wells and Rusthall Commons

Toad Rock and Rusthall, c.1913

A similar view, March 2000.

A History and Natural History

is exposed at Philpots Quarry (West Hoathly), the last active stone quarry in the Wealden. Quaternary silt deposits (brickearth) such as at Rusthall and Culverden Down have yielded stone age flint tools in the past.

Wealden iron.

The presence of workable iron ore and ancient woodland to make the charcoal fuel enabled iron smelting and casting in the Weald from prehistoric times. Indeed, the industry was only superseded by coke-fired processes developed in the Midlands during the Industrial Revolution. Much of the Wealden iron was obtained from siderite (iron carbonate) nodules in the Wadhurst Clay Formation. The history of this extinct industry, which predates the scientific study of geology, has received much attention from archaeologists and historians as well as geologists (see Cleere and Crossley 1995).

Places to visit.

These range from public open spaces to working quarries around Royal Tunbridge Wells. Conditions are liable to change and two recent field guides are Ruffell, Ross and Taylor (1996) for geology and Robinson and Williams (1984) for geomorphology. Health and safety considerations should be respected, especially on active sites. The conservation needs of the High Weald are summarized by Patmore (1997).

Tunbridge Wells and Rusthall Commons

A NEW WEALDEN FOSSIL LACEWING
Ed Jarzembowski

With their prominent eyespots and wingspans of up to approximately 250 mm., the extinct Kalligrammatidae – lacewings – were amongst the more spectacular insects from the Mesozoic age of the dinosaurs. Laurentiaux (1953) commented: 'on peut paralléliser leur rôle pictural à celui des papillons supérieurs dans la faune actuelle'. In other words, they were the 'butterflies' of dinosaur times. The only British record of the family is an incomplete wing from the Wadhurst Clay at Quarry Hill, Tonbridge, Kent. This specimen was reported by Roy Crowson (1946) and is the first fossil lacewing to be formally described and named from Kent.

Order Neuroptera Linnaeus 1758
Family Kalligrammatidae Handlirsh 1906 (not Kalligrammidae Handlirsch 1906, justified emendation of incorrect original spelling, Martynova, 1962)
Genus *Kalligramma* Walther 1904
Type species – *Kalligramma haeckeli* Walther 1904; Upper Jurassic, Solnhofen, Bavaria.

Kalligramma roycrowsoni sp. nov.
Kalligrammatid Jarzembowski, 1984: 82; fig. 36, pl. III.
Diagnosis – Early Cretaceous species differing from *Kalligramma multinerve* Panfilov in that the eyespot is larger but encompasses fewer (three) longitudinal veins.
Name – After the late Dr Roy A. Crowson, coleopterist and natural scientist associated with Royal Tunbridge Wells.
Description – The species is known from a single specimen, a fragment of a right wing including most of the eyespot and some adjacent parts of the wing. Comparison with the venation of *K. haeckeli* shows that parts of veins Rs, MA and MP are preserved, and from their convexities and concavities it is a right wing. MA is represented by part of the stem and two anteriorly directed branches. The posterior branch of MP has at least two posteriorly directed branches. There are numerous crossveins more or less perpendicular to the main veins except at the eyespot where the crossveins are intertwined. Traces of small hairs (microtrichia) occur on a few crossveins. The eyespot consists of a round black spot (pupil) surrounded by a lighter area (iris) which is itself bound by a brown ring. Further out are fainter and relatively diffuse concentric bands. Near the centre of the eyespot are four oval swellings.
Holotype – Department of Palaeontology, Natural History Museum, London. Specimen registration no. In. 48250. R. A. Crowson, collector.

A History and Natural History

Horizon and locality – 'Tilgate Stone,' Wadhurst Clay Formation, Quarry Hill, Tonbridge, Kent. National Grid Reference TQ 585 450.

Dimensions – Wing fragment: maximum length 32 mm., width 33 mm. Eyespot: mean diameter of pupil 8.0 mm.; mean diameter of iris 14.0 mm.

Remarks – Although fragmentary, the size of the wing, preserved venation, and form of the eyespot closely match those of the genus *Kalligramma* (Martynova 1962, fig. 865a; Panfilov 1968, fig. 2). The eyespot especially resembles that of *K. multinerve*, known from a single forewing from the Upper Jurassic of Karatau (Panfilov 1968). The Asian species also has a well-defined pupil surrounded by a ringed iris and incomplete concentric bands further out. Unfortunately, the posterior part of the eyespot of *K. multinerve* and much of the posterior part of the wing are not preserved. However, there is enough to show that the eyespot extends over more longitudinal veins (at least five) than in *Kalligramma roycrowsoni* sp. nov. The eyespot of *K. multinerve* is smaller, the pupil and iris being about 5.3 mm. and 10.6 mm. in diameter, respectively, judging from Panfilov's figures. The details of the eyespot in *K. haeckeli*, the type species, are poorly preserved (Walther 1904) as might be expected in fossil insects from the Solnhofen Limestone; for whilst they are often complete, they are nevertheless usually oxidised. What the Wealden specimen lacks in completeness is compensated for by the detailed preservation.

Tunbridge Wells and Rusthall Commons

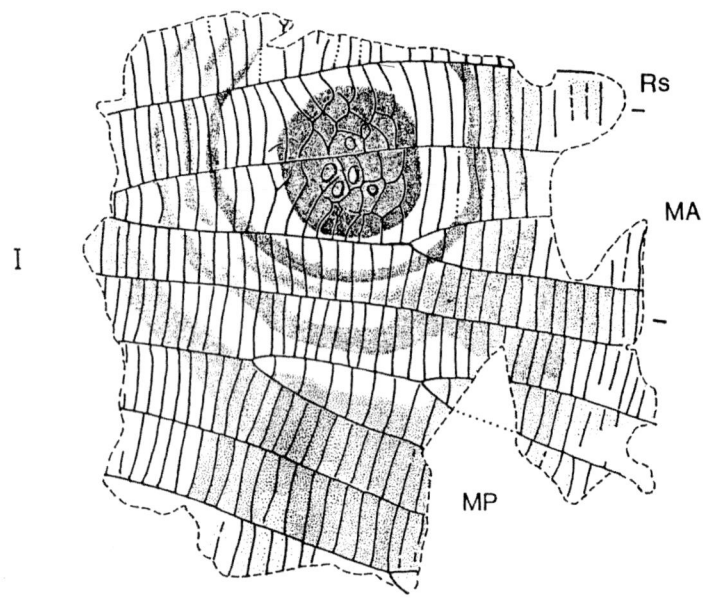

Venation and colour pattern of *Kalligramma roycrowsoni* sp. nov., unique type. Scale line = 1 mm.

Restoration drawing of *Kalligramma roycrowsoni* sp. nov. in flight

A History and Natural History

Wellington Rocks and the Wellington Hotel, *c.*1905

A similar view, March 2000

Tunbridge Wells and Rusthall Commons

Hoverfly *Volucella pellucens*

Swallow-tailed Moth

A History and Natural History

Flower beetle *Oedemera nobilis*

Peacock butterfly

Small Tortoiseshell butterfly

Female Common Blue butterfly

Tunbridge Wells and Rusthall Commons

Azure Damselfly

Nomad bee *Nomada goodeniana*

A History and Natural History

ANIMALS OF THE COMMONS
Ian Beavis

The 256 acres of Tunbridge Wells and Rusthall Commons provide an important and most unusual refuge for wildlife within the urban area. Unlike most public open spaces, they have never been landscaped or cultivated. This is not to suggest that they are pristine wild countryside, something which in any case does not exist in present day England. They owe much of their present appearance to human activity, and active management is required to maintain them in a fashion beneficial to their natural inhabitants. But the Commons nonetheless represent a genuinely ancient landscape, which long ago achieved a state of equilibrium between the needs of humanity and nature.

At the end of the last Ice Age, as temperate conditions reasserted themselves, the vast expanse of the primeval Wealden forest gradually came into existence. Within the forest, open heathy areas would have become established on thin soils, quite probably around the rock outcrops which brought the present Commons to the attention of their prehistoric inhabitants. Deliberate clearance of the forest cover, for hunting purposes, may have taken place as early as the Mesolithic, some 7,000 years ago. This would have transformed the Commons into a mixture of open grassland and heathland, with heather and gorse the most conspicuous vegetation, as they remained until the early twentieth century.

Deliberate planting of commemorative and ornamental trees, mainly between 1860 and 1940, led unintentionally to the re-establishment of woodland, as the traditional practice of grazing declined and finally ceased altogether in the inter-war period of the twentieth century. The Commons today consist of a mosaic of habitats, in which surviving areas of heath and grassland, along with the open sandy areas around the major rock formations, coexist with tracts of secondary woodland. Further diversity is provided by a series of semi-natural ponds. Current management aims to preserve this diversity, and a reasonable balance of the different elements, by containing the spread of woodland and expanding the open areas.

The present conservation management programme on the two Commons continues to improve them as a habitat for wildlife, and the long-established resident butterflies and dragonflies are flourishing in consequence. In addition, new species continue to appear. Some of these may have been present all along, but previously in such small numbers as to escape detection, but others are evidently new visitors or colonists for which conditions have now become suitable. It is fortunate for the Commons that the development of Tunbridge Wells has never cut them off completely from access to the open countryside. If they had become isolated islands in an urban landscape, it would have been

Tunbridge Wells and Rusthall Commons

much more difficult for wildlife from outside to reach them. Tunbridge Wells Common is open on its western boundary to the woodlands and meadows of the county border, and these same extensive habitats are adjacent to the southern edge of Rusthall Common.

The Commons have been noted for many years as a good spot for bird watching, bearing in mind their urban location and relatively small size. In the early 1960s local ornithologist Harold Betteridge listed thirty-six species nesting on the Commons, and made a photographic record of their nests. Nowadays, around forty resident species can be found, along with about fifteen summer or winter visitors. Familiar garden birds such as the Robin, Chaffinch, Blue Tit, Great Tit and Wren may readily be seen, and there are also records of more elusive relatives like the Bullfinch, Hawfinch, Goldcrest, Linnet and Redpoll. The large numbers of Magpies cannot fail to be observed, and their relatives the Carrion Crow, Jackdaw and Jay are also to be found. One of the most characteristic of the resident species is the Long-tailed Tit, often seen in small flocks moving from tree to tree; its elaborate nests of moss, spider webs and hair, covered with lichen, are constructed in gorse bushes. Groups of the colourful Goldfinch may be observed on occasions feeding at thistle seeds in large stands such as that beneath Mount Edgcumbe Rocks. The Song Thrush finds abundant snails of various species on the Commons, and its characteristic 'anvils', stones arising from bare ground and surrounded by shell fragments, can often be spotted along footpaths. The Mistle Thrush is also resident. The Nuthatch and Treecreeper inhabit the various wooded areas, where the occasional Pheasant has also been seen. Nightingales have been confirmed as nesting on Tunbridge Wells Common in the past, and adult birds continue to be reported.

The three British species of woodpecker are all to be found on the Commons, although the Great Spotted and Lesser Spotted are much less conspicuous than the Green. The latter has been noted feeding at anthills in the grassland near Wellington Rocks. Among the birds of prey, examples of the Kestrel and Sparrowhawk have been observed actively hunting in recent times, the former in open spots and the latter in more wooded areas. The Little Owl, Tawny Owl, and Long-eared Owl also have recent records. Few water birds occur on the Commons, but Mallard and Moorhen may be seen at Brighton Lake, and a Kingfisher has been spotted there recently. Summer visitors to the Commons include the ubiquitous Cuckoo, generally heard rather than seen, as well as the Spotted Flycatcher, Chiffchaff, Willow Warbler, Wood Warbler, Garden Warbler and Blackcap. Swallows and House Martins are to be seen hunting insects over open ground such as that between Victoria Grove and Wellington Rocks. Winter visitors include the Fieldfare and the Redwing.

A full list of mammals has yet to be compiled, but several species occur in

A History and Natural History

Nest and eggs of a Linnet (above) and Nightingale (below) on Tunbridge Wells Common. Photographs by Harold Betteridge from his 1962-4 Tunbridge Wells Common album

Tunbridge Wells and Rusthall Commons

addition to the substantial populations of grey squirrels and rabbits. Foxes are often to be seen, even in daylight, while badgers forage on the Commons at night from sets situated around the perimeter. Small deer undoubtedly occur on both Commons, although it is unclear whether they are a permanent feature or occasional visitors from the contiguous open countryside. Roe Deer have been seen on Rusthall Common, and there is also evidence for the introduced Muntjac. Mole hills are a familiar feature of some grassy areas such as that near Brighton Lake, and hedgehogs are also resident. Weasels have been recorded on Tunbridge Wells Common, and a Common Dormouse near Toad Rock. The areas of acid grassland with their tussocks and anthills are ideal for small rodents to feed while keeping themselves hidden from predators: voles, mice and shrews all occur, although particular species have not been identified. In the evening bats may be seen, mostly the Pipistrelle, a small and very common species, although the larger Noctule has also been reported.

The heathland environment of the Commons, along with their various ponds, have historically supported a variety of reptiles and amphibians. Despite the more recent decline of heathland, species such as the Common Lizard have managed to survive in more open areas. Lizards are seen quite regularly sunning themselves on anthills or similar exposed situations, although they are easily disturbed and rapidly vanish out of sight among the grass. They are most likely to be spotted in the grassland near Highbury or along Mount Ephraim. The Slow Worm, a legless lizard, has also been recorded, but is much more elusive. Another conspicuous reptile is the Grass Snake, which is most often seen near water. It can swim very effectively, and is regularly seen doing so in Brighton Lake. The Adder, a characteristic heathland species, is much less likely to be observed. The most widespread and abundant amphibians are the Common Frog and Common Toad, which breed prolifically in all the ponds on both Commons. The adults may be seen quite some distance from water. The three British species of newts are also found breeding in ponds on the Commons, although the rarer Great Crested is more restricted than the Smooth and Palmate.

Fish occur only in Brighton Lake, where they must originally have been introduced, as this pond was only created in 1858. However, they undoubtedly flourish there, and some surprisingly large specimens are in evidence. The population of sizable Carp is the most conspicuous, but Perch, Tench, Roach and Rudd are also present. A small Pike was recorded recently. Sticklebacks are also to be found.

The most prominent and widespread members of the Commons' insect fauna are the butterflies, of which twenty-five species have been recorded to date. Some are permanent residents, sedentary species with old established

A History and Natural History

colonies breeding on site generation after generation, while other more mobile species are regular or occasional visitors. The majority of the permanent residents are species characteristic of open grassland and heathland, and at their appropriate season most of them can be seen in areas such as (on Tunbridge Wells Common) the acid grassland along Mount Ephraim and overlooking London Road, the vicinity of Gibraltar Cottage, the north-west corner, and the space between Wellington Rocks and Victoria Grove; and (on Rusthall Common) Denny Bottom, and the grassland at the north-west corner, around the Marl Pits and in front of Rusthall Church. Such butterflies avoid dense woodland, but can be quite numerous along the open fringes of the wider footpaths like Pope's Terrace Walk.

The earliest of the grassland species to appear is the Small Copper, with its distinctive metallic orange colouration. Emerging in May, it is also one of the latest butterflies to remain on the wing in autumn. The Common Blue also has an early generation, and it too can appear remarkably late in the year. The period from June to August exhibits the greatest diversity of grassland butterflies, with the appearance of five warmth-loving species that produce only a single generation of adults each year, and whose caterpillars feed on grasses. The Small Skipper and Essex Skipper are the most difficult of British butterflies to distinguish, but can be reliably told apart by the tips of their antennae which are orange underneath in the former and black in the latter. The Large Skipper differs in size, as its name suggests, and has an orange patch on the forewing against a darker background. The Meadow Brown and the smaller Hedge Brown or Gatekeeper are characterized by small eyespots and light forewing patches on a darker brown background. Currently much scarcer than any of these is the Small Heath, a light orange-brown butterfly related to the two Browns but considerably smaller. The recently discovered Brown Argus, recorded only twice, is perhaps best interpreted as an elusive resident. A small brown butterfly with orange spots along the edges of its wings, it is easily mistaken for the female of the Common Blue, but the latter always has at least some blue scales, if only towards the base of its wings.

A common resident with somewhat different habitat preferences is the Speckled Wood, a distinctive butterfly with cream-white patches on a dark brown background which can be found from as early as April to as late as October. Although it breeds in open spots, its larvae feeding on grasses, the adults tend to frequent shady paths through woodland where the males defend territories consisting of a shifting patch of sunlight. The Purple Hairstreak is a much more elusive woodland resident, as the adult spends most of its life high in the branches of oak trees, where it feeds on honeydew. Its whole history centres around oaks, the eggs being laid on the leaf buds and the

Tunbridge Wells and Rusthall Commons

caterpillars feeding on the young foliage in spring. This butterfly is characterized by its metallic purple forewing patches, but it is rarely seen at close quarters. The Ringlet, a blackish brown butterfly with distinctive cream-coloured rings on its underside, was first recorded on the Commons in the mid-1990s and may well become a permanent resident. It is most likely to be seen in summer at brambles along rides and woodland edges.

There are a number of more mobile butterflies which regularly breed on the Commons and can be counted as residents, although they are active over a wider area, and individuals move in and out from urban parks and gardens and the adjacent countryside. One familiar group of three species whose larvae feed on nettles are among the first butterflies to appear in spring, as they hibernate as adults on site, concealing themselves in hollow trees and other sheltered spots, from which they emerge on the first warm sunny day of the year. The bright orange Small Tortoiseshell and the Peacock with its multi-coloured eyespots are familiar garden butterflies, but they are equally at home in such wild habitats as are found on the Commons, particularly in more open areas. The Comma, an orange-brown butterfly with irregular outlines to its wings, has a preference for more sheltered spots, favouring wide rides and woodland edges and in the autumn often feeding at ripe fruits like blackberries.

Late April sees the emergence of the distinctive Orange-tip, whose bright orange eggs are surprisingly easy to spot on their main foodplant, Garlic Mustard. Only the males have orange-tipped forewings, the females being mainly white, but sharing the same mottled green hindwing underside pattern. In flight, female Orange-tips closely resemble the Green-veined White, but when settled the latter's grey-green veins on the light yellowish hindwing underside are distinctive enough. Unlike the Orange-tip, which has only a single spring generation, the Green-veined White can be found throughout the year. Also present from spring to autumn is the Holly Blue, whose plain silver-white underside with a few black specks is the most obvious feature distinguishing it from the Common Blue. Its larvae feed on holly and ivy, and examples are generally seen along rides and woodland edges where its foodplants grow, rather than in the open areas frequented by its relative.

The lemon yellow males of the Brimstone are a familiar sight on the Commons in early spring. They hibernate as adults and generally appear at the same time as the Small Tortoiseshell, Peacock and Comma, ranging over a wide area. The Large White and Small White are also highly mobile species, their British populations regularly augmented by migration across the Channel. Both are frequently seen on the Commons, and the latter may sometimes breed there on wild members of the cabbage family. The familiar Red Admiral, patterned in white and scarlet on black, is similar to the Small Tortoiseshell

A History and Natural History

and Peacock in its habits and also breeds on nettles, but as it rarely survives the English winter it is not a permanent resident. Its population too is reinforced each year by migrants. The salmon pink Painted Lady is a much less regular migrant, although in favourable summers it has been recorded on the Commons in considerable numbers.

Day-flying moths can often be confused with butterflies, and some are surprisingly brightly coloured. A characteristically early species is the Orange Underwing, which flies in March and April, sunning itself with outspread wings on the ground in the wider footpaths or feeding at sallow catkins. May sees the appearance of the Small Yellow Underwing, a grassland species. The brilliant red and black Cinnabar moth is occasionally seen on the Commons, as is its distinctive orange and black striped caterpillar feeding on ragwort. In high summer, the Six-spot Burnet can sometimes be found flying in open grassland on both Commons, together with various butterflies. This moth has a similar colour scheme to the Cinnabar, but it is distinguished by the array of red spots on a forewing that is black with metallic reflections. These patterns are examples of warning colouration, which vertebrate predators learn to associate with creatures that are distasteful. The Silver Y is a much duller coloured insect, although its intricate pattern incorporating the metallic mark from which it takes its name is attractive on close inspection. Although sharing the nocturnal flight pattern of the majority of moths, the Silver Y is often active during the day as well, feeding at heather and other flowers. The metallic Green Longhorn and its relatives are much smaller insects, but the males with their astonishingly long antennae make themselves conspicuous in spring by flying in dancing swarms around sunlit trees and bushes.

The majority of the moths which live and breed on the Commons are purely nocturnal, and are therefore rarely or never seen by the general public. However, the use of a light trap at a number of locations, mainly on Tunbridge Wells Common, on several nights through 1992 produced a list of over one hundred and fifty species. It is certain that further and more regular trapping would increase the list considerably, and it is likely that most of the six hundred or so moth species recorded from Tunbridge Wells in modern times could be found on the Commons. Although moths have a reputation for being drab and nondescript insects, they are actually extremely diverse in colour and pattern, and a number of those recorded from the Commons are visually impressive creatures. Among the largest are the hawk moths, including the delicately patterned green Lime Hawk, the Poplar Hawk, and the brilliantly coloured pink and green Elephant Hawk. The latter takes its name from the resemblance of its caterpillar, found on willow-herb, to an elephant's trunk. As its name suggests, the White Ermine is pure white with scattered black spots, while its relative, the Buff Ermine, has a similar pattern but different

Tunbridge Wells and Rusthall Commons

ground colour. When its wings are folded the Buff-tip has a remarkable resemblance to a broken silver birch twig, while the related Swallow Prominent and Lesser Swallow Prominent have streamlined wings with an elegant white and brown pattern. The Brimstone moth, with bright yellow wings, shares its name with a butterfly, as does the Swallow-tailed, a large broad-winged insect of a delicate yellowish shade. Other strikingly coloured species include the Peach Blossom, the Light Emerald, and the bright metallic Burnished Brass.

Brighton Lake, Fir Tree Pond and Bracken Cottage Pond (on Tunbridge Wells Common) and the Marl Pits (on Rusthall Common) all support breeding colonies of dragonflies, although the larger spring-fed Brighton Lake is the most productive. The early stages or nymphs of these insects live as predators underwater, and adult females can often be seen laying their eggs by dipping the tip of their abdomen into the water. Regular breeding species include a number of damselflies, the smaller members of the dragonfly order, of which the most numerous are the distinctive Large Red, first to appear in spring, the Blue-tailed, and the Common Blue and Azure, which resemble each other very closely. The scarce White-legged Damselfly, creamy white in colour, is less often seen. Damselflies fly together, often in large numbers, as does the medium-sized Common Darter, which is the last to emerge and continues to be active well into November, long after most other insects have ceased to appear. In contrast, the larger dragonflies, of which the commonest are the Emperor, the Broad-bodied Chaser, the Southern Hawker and the Brown Hawker, live a mostly solitary existence. They are fiercely territorial, with individuals commanding a small pond or part of a larger one and driving off any potential rivals. In total, seventeen species of dragonflies have been recorded from the Commons to date, although a number of these are only occasional residents or strays from richer localities on the Sussex border. Such visitors include the Downy Emerald, the Banded Demoiselle, and the magnificent Gold-ringed Dragonfly, the largest British species.

Grasshoppers and crickets form a prominent part of the Commons' insect fauna, particularly in high summer when the distinctive songs of a number of species can be heard throughout the areas of open grass and heathland. These songs are a means of communication between the sexes, and can be recognized in the same way as bird song. Most of the sound to be heard in summer grassland emanates from the Commons' three grasshopper species: the Common Field Grasshopper and Common Green Grasshopper, both of which are fully winged, and the short-winged Meadow Grasshopper. Of the bush-crickets, the only one with an audible song is the Long-winged Conehead, a former rarity which has only recently colonized the Tunbridge Wells area. The Dark Bush-cricket and Speckled Bush-cricket live in dense vegetation such as bramble thickets and may be spotted sitting on leaves. The delicate

A History and Natural History

pale green Oak Bush-cricket spends its time high in the trees and is only occasionally seen at ground level, when for example it is blown down by the wind. The Common and Slender Ground-hopper are generally inconspicuous creatures that can sometimes be spotted in numbers on sparsely vegetated ground, often near water.

Walkers on the Commons in high summer will undoubtedly have seen clusters of small holes in the sandy ground of footpaths and around rocks, and may well have spotted insects of various sizes and colours, looking vaguely like bees and wasps, going in and out of them. The more observant may have noticed similar burrows in south-facing drainage ditches, root plates or banks with sparse vegetation from early spring onwards. These small tunnels are the nests of solitary bees and wasps, an often overlooked but important element of the Commons' fauna. The sandy soil and rock outcrops of the Commons are ideal for these creatures, and many otherwise rare varieties find a refuge here. Over one hundred and thirty species have so far been recorded, including eighteen on the official national list of scarce and endangered species.

Solitary bees and wasps are so called to distinguish them from their 'social' relatives which live in communities with a breeding queen and sterile workers. Although solitary species often nest in close proximity, congregating in particularly favoured spots, each female digs its own individual burrow and stocks it with suitable food for its offspring. The earliest species to appear are the mining bees, some of which can be active even in late February while most are at their peak in March and April. The females dig burrows in bare or sparsely vegetated ground, which they stock with honey and pollen before laying their eggs. They are especially fond of south-facing areas such as Pope's Terrace Walk, the back of Brighton Lake, and Happy Valley. Wellington Rocks and the rocks at Denny Bottom are also favoured sites. Laying in a store of food for their offspring entails numerous visits to and from nearby flowers, so the females can often be seen entering their tunnels carrying clumps of brightly coloured pollen in the baskets of hairs on their hind legs. Mining bees are very diverse in size and colour, the largest being about the size of a honey bee, while the smallest are not much bigger than a large ant. The most spectacular, the Tawny Mining Bee (*Andrena fulva*), has bright orange fur on its hind body, while the thorax is deep scarlet. Other species frequently observed in spring include the Early Mining Bee (*A. haemorrhoa*), which has a golden tip to its body, the Yellow-legged Mining Bee (*A. flavipes*), which has a golden pollen basket and pale brown bands, and the very early flying *Andrena clarkella*, with black fur behind and red in front. Among the few which fly in summer is the white-banded *Colletes succinctus*, always seen visiting heather. Female mining bees are generally more distinctive than males, but the light grey males of *Andrena barbilabris* often make themselves

Tunbridge Wells and Rusthall Commons

conspicuous by flying low over areas of bare sand.

Female mining bees often make great efforts to conceal their nests from predators, carefully opening and sealing them as they travel to and fro with supplies. However, this does not protect them from the cuckoo bees whose females are highly skilled in detecting other bees' burrows so that they can lay their own eggs inside and save themselves the trouble of gathering their own stores of food. Every species of mining bee has a particular specialist cuckoo species which is attached to it, roaming around its nesting sites in search of opportunities. The smaller mining bees have associated cuckoos of the genus *Sphecodes*, which are red and black in colour, but the larger varieties are parasitized by the more conspicuous nomad bees. The nomad bees, which can often be seen in spring exploring the areas where mining bees congregate, have a close resemblance to wasps. One of the commonest, the Red-horned Nomad (*Nomada flava*), has yellow, black and brown bands, and three vertical red stripes on the thorax. The body of the larger Six-banded Nomad (*N. fulvicornis*), one of the Commons' rarities, is patterned entirely in yellow and black.

Later in the year, the mining bees are joined by various smaller groups, some of which make their nests in rotten wood. The Red Carpenter Bee (*Osmia rufa*) has light orange fur on its abdomen, while the Blue Carpenter Bee (*O. coerulescens*) is of a dark metallic colour. The females of the Commons' three species of leaf-cutter bees (*Megachile* spp.) use their powerful jaws to cut semicircular pieces out of leaves. They use these to make a series of individual cells in their burrows, filling them with honey and pollen for their young. The pieces of leaf are folded into a cylinder, with smaller round portions serving as a base and lid. Female leaf-cutters have a rather flattened body with a brush of coloured hairs underneath for carrying pollen. The scarce flower bee *Anthophora quadrimaculata*, which resembles a small brown bumblebee with a swift darting flight, is exclusively devoted to flowers of the labiate family, which it visits in company with the larger orange-tailed *A. furcata* and the yellow-spotted Wool-carder Bee (*Anthidium manicatum*).

Solitary wasps do not generally become active until June or later. Many species nest in similar locations to those favoured by mining bees, while others burrow into dead wood and can be found exploring sunlit timber. In contrast to the bees, these wasps provide live food for their young. The largest group, the digger wasps, show a wide range of size and colour pattern, some having the typical wasp pattern of yellow and black stripes, while other species are red and black, or all black. The nesting females capture flies, beetles, caterpillars or other insects, according to the preference of each species. They prepare their captures for use by the expedient of paralysing them with their sting, so that the victims remain fresh but unable to escape from the burrow

A History and Natural History

while the wasp larva hatches from its egg and begins to devour them. Among the more conspicuous ground-nesting species, with substantial colonies around Wellington Rocks and Toad Rock, are the yellow and black *Cerceris arenaria*, which hunts for weevils, and the red and black *Astata boops*, whose prey is shield bug nymphs. The large but scarce Red-banded Sand Wasp (*Ammophila sabulosa*) seeks out caterpillars, and is notable for its amazingly long and slender 'wasp waist'. The spider-hunting wasps (Pompilidae), red and black or all black in colour, have similar habits to the digger wasps, but specialize in the capture of spiders. They are agile and fast-moving insects which run rather than fly as they seek out their prey.

As with solitary bees, the digger wasps and spider-hunting wasps have their associated cuckoo species which intrude into their stocked nests and lay their eggs there. These parasites include several species of ruby wasps, which are among the most attractive and exotic-looking of British insects. They are active only in bright sunshine and are brilliantly metallic, coloured in various combinations of green, ruby red and deep blue. The most beautiful of all, *Chrysis viridula*, is most often seen on Rusthall Common, exploring the nesting sites of its host the Spiny Mason Wasp (*Odynerus spinipes*), which is distinctive in its own right by reason of the curious curved mud chimneys which it constructs over the entrance to its burrows in bare vertical sandy surfaces.

Although numerically abundant, social bees and wasps are much fewer in number of species than their solitary cousins. On the Commons, the most widespread are six species of bumblebees, whose furry coat enables them to fly in cold, dull or rainy weather when most other insects are immobilized. Like all insects that live in colonies, each species is divided into three castes: queens, males and workers. The queens are the fertile females and founders of the colony, surviving the winter by hibernation and emerging as early as possible in the new year to establish their nests, either in holes in the ground or in dense vegetation. The nest consists of a ball of dried grass or moss, in the centre of which the female builds wax cells for her eggs, along with containers for storing food. Her first offspring are workers, sterile females which assist in the development of the colony and take over the work of gathering nectar and pollen. The Buff-tailed (*Bombus terrestris*), White-tailed (*B. lucorum*), Garden (*B. hortorum*), Early (*B. pratorum*) and Red-tailed (*B. lapidarius*) Bumblebee are all familiar visitors to flowers on the Commons, as is the distinctive brown Common Carder Bee (*B. pascuorum*). Lone queens seen flying low in the early months of the year are engaged in their search for suitable nest sites. Honeybees are regularly seen on the Commons too, but these are visitors from domestic hives. Social wasps recorded on the Commons comprise the two familiar urban species *Vespula vulgaris* and *V. germanica*, along with the Tree Wasp (*Dolichovespula sylvestris*) and two related species

Tunbridge Wells and Rusthall Commons

which have recently colonized southern Britain from the Continent (*D. media* and *D. saxonica*).

The other social insects found on the Commons are the ants, one of which contributes a major feature to the landscape in the form of the prominent earthen mounds to be seen in areas of acid grassland such as that around Highbury. These are constructed by the Yellow Meadow Ant (*Lasius flavus*), and may be many decades old. The ants themselves remain below the surface and are unlikely to be seen unless one of their nests is disturbed. Sections of these old nest mounds are sometimes occupied by colonies of the brown ant *Myrmica scabrinodis*. Unlike the meadow ant, this and its relative *M. ruginodis* are commonly seen actively foraging, often high up on grassland vegetation. Most widespread of all, found both in open spots and in woodland, are the familiar subterranean nesting Black Garden Ant (*Lasius niger*) and the larger long-legged *Formica fusca*. It is the Black Garden Ant whose winged females are most likely to be noticed by the general public as swarms of 'flying ants' on hot days in high summer. These are newly emerged queens engaged, along with the much smaller males, in their annual synchronized courtship flight, after which they shed their wings to retreat underground as founders of new colonies.

Numerous as they are, bees, wasps and ants form only part of Britain's largest order of insects, the Hymenoptera. The other members of the order are also well represented on the Commons, but most are small and inconspicuous. Several species of sawflies, however, are quite large and brightly coloured, and may be seen visiting flowers. Their name derives from the females' saw-like ovipositor, used to insert their eggs within plant tissues. Many sawflies have larvae which feed openly on leaves and resemble the caterpillars of moths and butterflies, but others develop inside galls which their foodplant produces in response to the larva's presence. Galls, which take distinctive forms according to the insect species that causes them, are also produced by the Cynipidae or gall wasps, and in this case they are much easier to identify than the minute insects themselves. Many cynipid galls can be found on the Commons, including the familiar oak apple, the marble and spangle galls, also on oak, and the robin's pincushion on rose. Another important group of Hymenoptera are the ichneumon flies, whose larvae feed as parasites inside caterpillars or other insects. The females are generally armed with a conspicuous ovipositor, and some of the larger species are brightly patterned in yellow and black or red and black. They are most often seen running about on sunlit foliage, or flying around bushes and low vegetation in search of suitable hosts.

Among the most prominent of the two-winged flies or Diptera are the hoverflies, named for their aerial skills which allow them to hang motionless

A History and Natural History

in mid-air. They are also effective mimics of bees and wasps. Young birds soon learn that insects patterned in yellow and black or red and black are either distasteful or capable of stinging, and many harmless insects gain protection by having a similar appearance. Around sixty species of hoverflies are to be found on the Commons, most of them visiting flowers along with their models. The largest British species belong to the genus *Volucella*, and the impressive *V. zonaria*, a migrant species, has occasionally been recorded on the Commons. More likely to be seen is *V. pellucens*, which regularly hovers along woodland paths; its black and white colouration, unusual among hoverflies, is shared by the smaller spring-flying *Leucozona lucorum*. The slender-bodied members of the genus *Xylota* are to be seen on sunlit leaves rather than flowers: they include the red-banded *X. segnis* and the beautiful gold-banded *X. sylvarum*. The droneflies, of which six species are found on the Commons, are bee mimics, and include the very common *Eristalis tenax*, which is notable for hibernating as an adult and appearing on sunny days all through the year. This species and the similar *E. pertinax* resemble honeybees, while *E. intricarius* is a furry bumblebee mimic. Many of the Commons' hoverflies have variations on the standard wasp pattern of yellow and black stripes. These include the common *Syrphus ribesii*, the distinctive *Helophilus pendulus* with vertical stripes on the thorax as well as the usual horizontal ones on the abdomen, and the latter's larger and scarcer relative *H. trivittatus*.

Robber flies are a group of fierce predators which capture smaller insects with their spiny fore-legs. A number, like the widespread *Machimus atricapillus*, are characteristic of open areas where they perch on bare sand, rocks or low vegetation, waiting for suitable victims. Other forms, such as the shiny black *Laphria marginata* and *Neoitamus cyanurus* with its metallic blue tail, are found in woodland areas and may be spotted on sunlit foliage beside footpaths. Much smaller predators are the long-headed flies, often metallic green or silvery in colour, many of which are also to be seen on sunlit foliage or around the edges of ponds. The males of the most conspicuous, *Poecilobothrus nobilitatus*, have white-tipped wings which are waved in its courtship display as large numbers of both sexes swarm over damp mud. Soldier flies are brightly coloured sun-loving insects, of which those found on the Commons include the metallic green *Chloromyia formosa* and the three-coloured *Sargus bipunctatus*. The bee-fly *Bombylius major*, as its name suggests, resembles a brown bumblebee, and is frequently seen in spring exploring the nest sites of solitary bees, in which its larvae live as parasites, or hovering in front of flowers and probing them with its long rigid proboscis.

The largest member of the Diptera found on the Commons is the impressive marbled-winged cranefly *Tipula maxima*. Craneflies, with their enormously long legs, are an easily recognized group of insects, and the familiar medium-

Tunbridge Wells and Rusthall Commons

sized forms, some patterned with yellow and black, are widespread in the grassy areas of the Commons, as is the shiny black St Mark's Fly (*Bibio marci*), named after its characteristic swarming flight in spring. The flies of the family Tachinidae spend their larval stage as internal parasites of other insects, usually caterpillars, but the bristly adults often feed conspicuously at flowers, and some are brightly coloured. One of the most numerous species on the Commons is the red-spotted *Eriothrix rufomaculatus* which can be found visiting ragwort. The beautifully metallic greenbottles (*Lucilia* spp.) are among the most abundant of many Diptera species which rest in open view on sunlit foliage and tree trunks; others include the shiny black *Mesembrina meridiana* with its bright yellow wing bases.

Numerous species of beetles occur on the Commons. Although the majority are inconspicuous creatures, there are some which by reason of their size or colour may bring themselves to the attention of the non-specialist. The majority of the fast-moving predatory ground beetles (Carabidae) are nocturnal, but a number of metallic brassy species make themselves conspicuous by running across sunlit paths. The related Green Tiger Beetle (*Cicindela campestris*), a brightly coloured species which flies readily in hot weather, is sometimes seen in similar situations. The ladybirds, whose bright colours advertise them as distasteful to birds, are also predators, feeding on aphids. Such species as the very common Seven-spot (*Coccinella septempunctata*) and smaller Two-spot (*Adalia bipunctata*) Ladybird hibernate as adults and may be in evidence on sunny days in winter. Aquatic predators include the impressive Great Diving Beetle (*Dytiscus marginalis*), found with many related forms in the various ponds on both Commons.

Many beetles feed on plant foliage, keeping themselves well hidden, but some of the Chrysomelidae or leaf beetles are brightly coloured, as are the metallic green leaf weevils (*Phyllobius* spp.) found on various trees and low-growing plants. The Variable Reed Beetle (*Plateumaris sericea*), found on emergent vegetation at the fringes of ponds, may be bronze, copper, deep blue or purple in colour. Of the beetles which feed actively at flowers, the most abundant is the soldier beetle *Rhagonycha fulva*, orange with black tips, a characteristic insect of high summer. Several related species occur in smaller numbers, all being particularly fond of the tall flower heads of umbellifers, thistles and ragwort. The red-tipped *Malachius bipustulatus* and the slender *Oedemera nobilis*, both metallic green, are more characteristic of low-growing flowers such as buttercups. The brilliant reflective scarlet of the Commons' two species of cardinal beetle (*Pyrochroa coccinea* and *P. serraticornis*) render them instantly noticeable, whether they are visiting flowers, sitting on foliage or in flight. Many of the longhorn beetles, noted for their conspicuous antennae, are strikingly coloured or patterned, flying on sunny days and feeding

A History and Natural History

at brambles and other flowers. They include the yellow and black Wasp Beetle (*Clytus arietis*) and Spotted Longhorn (*Strangalia maculata*), and two larger orange and black species, *S. quadrifasciata* and the rare and impressive *S. aurulenta*.

Rove beetles, characterized by their short wing cases exposing most of the abdomen, are abundant inhabitants of the Commons, although most species are small and do not attract attention. Only the large black *Staphylinus olens*, the so-called Devil's Coach-horse, is likely to be noticed by the general public running over sunlit footpaths. Click beetles, slender insects so called because of their ability to flip themselves upright after falling on their backs, are also numerous, and the common *Athous haemorrhoidalis* actively flies by day. The large mottled *Agrypnus murinus* is another notable member of the same family. Members of the scarab group found on the Commons include the familiar Cockchafer or May-bug (*Melolontha melolontha*), which is nocturnal and attracted to light, the Minotaur Beetle (*Typhaeus typhoeus*), a dung-beetle with three horns in the male, and the Lesser Stag Beetle (*Dorcus parallelipipedus*).

The extensive order Hemiptera is divided into two sections, the true bugs or Heteroptera and the aphids, leafhoppers, froghoppers and related forms of the sub-order Homoptera. An often overlooked group of insects, many species are found in grassland and woodland on the Commons. The Homoptera are mostly small insects which attract little attention, although the nymphs of froghoppers reveal their presence by producing protective 'cuckoo spit', in which they are concealed, and some aphids feed in large clusters which are attended by ants in search of honeydew. Some of the larger and more colourful leafhoppers may also be noticed by the non-specialist, for example the bright green *Cicadella viridis* which frequents the damp grassland around ponds. Among the largest of the true bugs found on the Commons are the shieldbugs, including the common Green Shieldbug (*Palomena prasina*), often seen on bramble foliage, and the attractive green and purple Hawthorn (*Acanthosoma haemorrhoidale*) and Birch (*Elasmostethus interstinctus*) Shieldbugs. The large brown squashbug *Coreus marginatus is* also easy to spot, as it sits openly on dock leaves. Aquatic members of the Heteroptera include the backswimmer *Notonecta glauca* and the familiar pond-skaters (*Gerris* spp.), which live on the surface film of ponds.

The ponds on the Commons also support various species of mayflies, stoneflies and caddis-flies. The larvae of the latter are well-known for the protective cases constructed by some species out of plant material or other debris gathered from their watery habitat, but the dull brown adults, if noticed at all, are likely to be mistaken for moths. These three groups are among the smaller insect orders, as are the lacewings, which are predatory on aphids in

Tunbridge Wells and Rusthall Commons

both adult and larval stages. Those most likely to be noted on the Commons are the delicate green species of the genus *Chrysopa*. A related group are the scorpion-flies, often seen fluttering among brambles or nettles. Despite the curious scorpion-like tail of the male, they are harmless scavengers.

In conclusion, brief mention should be made of invertebrate groups other than insects. On the Commons, the spiders are the most conspicuous of these, representing a variety of lifestyles. Spiders are most popularly associated with the building of webs, the most elaborate being those constructed by the orb weavers such as the large and familiar *Araneus diadematus* or the smaller bright green *Araniella cucurbitina*. Many species, however, actively hunt their prey. These include the jumping spiders (Salticidae), often seen on sunlit rocks, the fast running wolf spiders (Lycosidae) which may be seen in large numbers on open ground, the females carrying their silken egg-sacks, and impressive white-striped *Pisaura mirabilis*, which is generally seen perched conspicuously on foliage. The white or yellow crab spider *Misumena vatia* sits on flowers waiting to pounce on visiting insects. Centipedes, millipedes and woodlice generally keep themselves out of sight under stones or fallen timber, although the shiny black cylindrical millipede *Tachypodoiulus niger* sometimes makes its presence more obvious by climbing the trunks of trees. The Pill Millipede (*Glomeris marginata*) defends itself by rolling into a ball, as does the superficially similar Pill Woodlouse (*Armadillidium vulgare*). Unlike the slower millipedes, centipedes are fast moving predators, the most distinctive species on the Commons being *Lithobius variegatus* with purple bands on its legs and similarly coloured marks on its body. Molluscs too are a significant element in the Commons' fauna, both in the various ponds and on land. The most attractive of the terrestrial snails is the highly variable *Cepaea hortensis*, whose brightly coloured or banded shells are often seen in fragmentary form around the 'anvils' of the Song Thrush.

A History and Natural History

PLANTS OF THE COMMONS
Mary Page

The area of Tunbridge Wells is well known for the rich variety of its flora and the Commons are no exception.

Throughout the year wild flowers can be found here. The Daisy (*Bellis perennis*) and the various species of dandelion (*Taraxacum* spp.) can be seen in any month from January to December, but it is not until early spring that a greater assortment come into flower with small plants making the most of their opportunities to blossom before the trees have opened their leaves.

Clumps of bright yellow petals shining like stars along the edges of woodland in early March are the flowers of the Lesser Celandine (*Ranunculus ficaria*). A member of the buttercup family, it was well known to the old herbalists who used it to cure various complaints. Much harder to find are the little inconspicuous white flowers of the Barren Strawberry (*Potentilla sterilis*), so called as it is sterile and not to be confused with the Wild Strawberry (*Fragaria vesca*), which appears later and whose fruits are the sweet tasting small strawberries of the summer. Lesser Periwinkle (*Vinca minor*), with its dark green shining leaves, now shows its not very numerous purple flowers. Its trailing stems were used in Roman times entwined in the victory laurel wreaths. Found on the edges of the woodland is the dainty Wood Anemone or Windflower (*Anemone nemorosa*) which has many associations with Greek mythology. Another flower of the spring woodland is the Wood Sorrel (*Oxalis acetosella*) with its shamrock-like leaves and delicate white flowers veined with mauve. Its leaves are very bitter but nevertheless eaten by country children and known as Bread and Cheese, and it has been used as a salad vegetable since the fourteenth century.

What of the trees of the spring? The Hazel (*Corylus avellana*) is perhaps the earliest to open its hanging catkins or 'lamb's tails' which can be scattering yellow pollen as early as January in a mild winter. Somewhere on the Commons in early April may be seen a cloud of white against the black branches, which is the blossom of the Blackthorn (*Prunus spinosa*), a tree from which our cultivated plums have been developed. It is named Blackthorn because it flowers before the leaves in contrast to the Whitethorn or Hawthorn. The other April flowering tree is Juneberry (*Amelanchier lamarckii*), an introduced tree, probably bird sown, which grows very quickly producing an attractive white blossom in loose clusters, followed by purplish berries. There is one old tree growing near the Wellington Rocks and quite a few younger ones scattered over the wooded area.

In May the apple trees in blossom are a most delightful sight with their pinkish white flowers covering the branches. The truly wild Crab Apple (*Malus*

Tunbridge Wells and Rusthall Commons

sylvestris) is not very common, but the Cultivated Apple (*Malus domestica*) is a frequent product of discarded apple cores and most, if not all, of the specimens on the Commons are of the latter variety. Introduced in the fifteenth century from the Near East is the Horse Chestnut (*Aesculus hippocastanum*), a distinctive tree at any season. At the beginning of the year the buds become very prominent, shiny and sticky and arranged in opposite pairs, which each have a horseshoe-shaped scar beneath them. As the buds open they develop five to seven leaflets which make up the compound leaf. These are then followed by the lovely upright clusters of white flowers dotted with crimson and yellow, which are often known as candles. Later in the year they become the fruits which so delight the children, the shiny polished-looking conkers. In April, the Blackthorn is out before the leaves and now in May the Whitethorn or Hawthorn (*Crataegus monogyna*) blossoms with the leaves. Although a very common tree indeed, it looks extremely beautiful with its branches full of flowers, which can be white or pink clusters, and heavily scented. These turn into the fruits of autumn, commonly known as haws. The old saying 'Cast ne'er a clout till May be out' refers to the flowering of the hawthorn and not to the month of May.

One of the first grasses in spring is the Wood Melick (*Melica uniflora*), which is very attractive with its bright green leaves and dainty nodding heads of egg-shaped, purple spikelets. It is often to be seen growing by the woodland edges along with Bluebells (*Hyacinthoides non-scripta*), too well known to need any description. Most people have picked bluebells and may remember that the stalks contain a sticky juice and this, in the sixteenth century, was made into a kind of starch. Gerard, a herbalist of the time, says that bluebell juice was also made into a glue which was used for sticking feathers on to arrows and in the ancient craft of bookbinding. There is another plant flowering at the same time as the Bluebell and that is the Wild Arum (*Arum maculatum*) which was also used to make starch. It has other names such as Cuckoo Pint, Lords and Ladies, and Jack in the Pulpit, but perhaps the best name of all is one which, according to Geoffrey Grigson (1955), was used in Kent. It is 'Kitty-come-down-the-lane-jump-up-and-kiss-me!' Gerard called it Starchwort and says 'the most pure and white starch is made out of the roots of Cuckoo Pint, but the most hurtful for the laundress that hath the handling of it, for it chappeth, blistereth and maketh the hands rough and rugged and withall smarting!' The fruits that appear later in the year are very attractive spikes of bright red berries, but they are very poisonous.

There are thirteen different violets in our flora; two grow on the Commons. The Wood Dog Violet (*Viola reichenbachiana*) starts blooming at the end of March and can be distinguished, by its unnotched dark purple spur, from the Common Dog Violet (*Viola riviniana*) which flowers about a fortnight later.

A History and Natural History

One of the most handsome of the violets, unfortunately, it has no scent, hence the name dog as a reproach.

Most of the rarities of the Commons are spring flowers. Firstly, the Coral Root (*Cardamine bulbifera*), a crucifer which is rare over most of the British Isles but grows profusely along the Kent and Sussex borders including wooded parts of the Commons. It looks similar to Ladies Smock or Milkmaids (*Cardamine pratensis*) which is a familiar plant found in the grassland, but there is a difference; at the base of the upper stem leaves of the Coral Root are small red bulbils, and it is these that fall to the ground to make new plants. Nearby the Star of Bethlehem (*Ornithogalum umbellatum*) a member of the lily family is another rarity. Although it was probably originally planted, it has been established where it now grows since before the Second World War. The flowers are large, white, open, umbel-like heads with a green stripe on the back of the six petals. Another lily growing on Rusthall Common, Solomon's Seal (*Polygonatum multiflorum*), is an unusual plant with its arching stems and bell-shaped flowers hanging from the base of the leaves. It is quite rare and not to be confused with the garden variety which is much bigger.

By mid-May there is a diversity of flowers growing in the open grassland and along the edges of the Common. Cow Parsley (*Anthriscus sylvestris*) of the umbellifer family with its umbels of creamy white flowers looking like a froth of white lace, is very attractive and because of this it has acquired a number of country names such as Queen Anne's Lace and Gypsy's Curtains which seem very appropriate. There is also a smaller umbellifer growing in the grass, Pignut or Earthnut (*Conopodium majus*). It is called Pignut because of the brown tubers at the end of the stalks known as 'nuts' by country children who enjoyed eating them. One Victorian botanist disapproved and wrote in a typically Victorian manner that 'the nuts were better fitted to the digestion of the respectable quadrupeds whose name they share than for Christian bipeds of tender years', but the children still ate them.

May is the month of the buttercups and all three of the best known can be found. First to bloom is the Bulbous Buttercup (*Ranunculus bulbosus*) so called because of the markedly swollen base to the stem. There is no need to dig up the plant to identify it, just look at the sepals, which turn down against the stem unlike the others which cling to the base of the petals. The Creeping Buttercup (*Ranunculus repens*) flowers next and looks quite attractive growing on the Common, but with its prolific rooting runners it is not at all popular in gardens where it can become a pernicious weed which is difficult to eradicate. The tallest and most graceful is the Meadow Buttercup (*Ranunculus acris*), which is the latest and is often seen in great quantity in the grass. Growing among the buttercups is Sorrel (*Rumex acetosa*), a plant long associated with old meadows. Its spike of rather insignificant flowers becomes more

Tunbridge Wells and Rusthall Commons

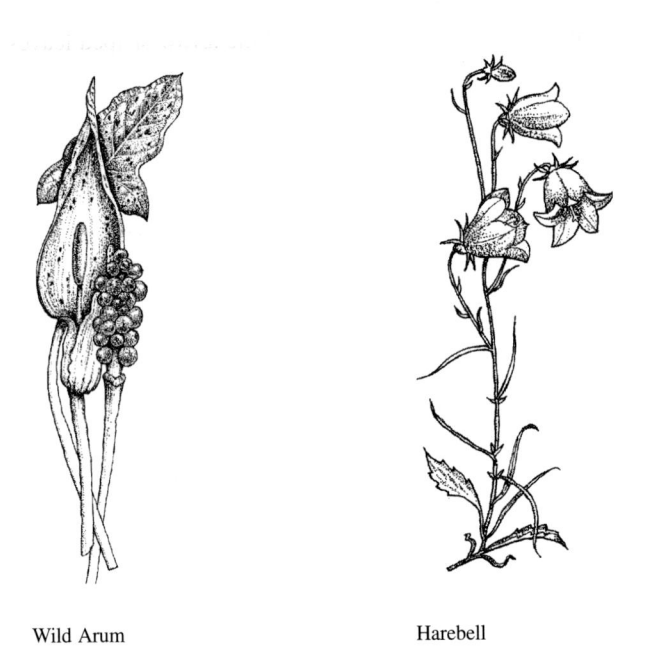

Wild Arum

Harebell

Water Crowfoot

A History and Natural History

prominent, reddening as the seeds open and males and females grow on separate plants. Sorrel means bitter and the arrow-shaped leaves have long been used as a culinary herb. Somewhere on the Commons in May can be found the Ox-Eye Daisy (*Leucanthemum vulgare*), also known as the Dog Daisy, Horse Daisy, Moon Daisy, and in Scotland the Gowan, but the prettiest name is Margeurite, named after the French Princess who married Henry VI in the fifteenth century. The daisy was her emblem and she had it embroidered on all her gowns. There are many superstitions attached to it. It was lucky to tread on the first flower of the season but unlucky to dig it up as that would lead to children or young animals growing up stunted. There are at least six speedwells on the Common, by far the most frequent being the Germander or Birdseye Speedwell (*Veronica chamaedrys*). It is a native and because of its bright blue flowers it has many country names such as Angels' Eyes or Kitty's Eyes. The petals fall quickly when touched and that has led to the name Mother Breaks Her Heart. In some places speedwell was sewn on to the clothes of travellers to keep them from accident and it was also put into the shoes of those going on a journey as it was said that with speedwell in your shoes you could walk ten miles without feeling tired.

Both well-known clovers are here. Red Clover (*Trifolium pratense*) is a native plant and was introduced into agriculture about 1645 when it was known as Marl Grass. It has a host of names such as Bee Bread and Honeystalks as it was one of the plants whose stalks were picked to suck the honey from the flowers. White Clover (*Trifolium repens*) is also a native connected with farming, which is sometimes called Dutch Clover as it was recognized in Holland many years ago as a valuable fodder plant. When the British farmers realized its worth, they imported a great quantity of seed from the Dutch. Both Red and White were known in the Middle Ages as Clavers and some say this refers to the trefoil (the three leaves) and comes from the Latin *clava* meaning club or cudgel, hence the three-knotted club of Hercules and the club of our playing cards.

Bird's Foot Trefoil (*Lotus corniculatus*), another peaflower, is a pretty, short and rather sprawling perennial with red and yellow petals, and seedheads resembling a bird's foot which has given rise to various names from Five Fingers to Crow's Feet. The flowers were also supposed to look like medieval shoes so Ladies Slipper and Socks and Shoes were used as well, and Eggs and Bacon and Ham and Eggs refer to the colours of the flowers. This plant is often found in the short grass. Talking of grasses, the Sweet Vernal Grass (*Anthoxanthum odorata*) can be seen in many places where the grass is short. Its name comes from the dried grass which is aromatic and popular for chewing. Cocksfoot (*Dactylis glomerata*), a perennial of rough grassland and notable for the cluster of spikelets said to look like a chicken's foot, is known in some

Tunbridge Wells and Rusthall Commons

places as Cutting Grass because when the stalks are pulled roughly they can give a nasty cut. The well-known and handsome Foxglove (*Digitalis purpurea*) is very eye-catching with its spike of large purplish flowers, spotted inside, hanging down tall stems. They somewhat resemble the fingers of a glove so names such as Granny's Gloves and Fairy's Thimbles are very apt. It is a biennial so for the first year only a tuft of lanceolate leaves is seen and it is the second year which produces the flowering stems. Although very poisonous, it is used medicinally in the treatment of heart disease. On the edges of Rusthall Common is the Greater Celandine (*Chelidonium majus*), no relation of the Lesser Celandine seen earlier. This plant belongs to the poppy family and has bright yellow flowers with four petals. The stalks contain a yellow juice and this was used to treat sore eyes as far back as Saxon times. The fact that it was so used may explain why it is always found near human habitation.

One of the features of the Commons are the ponds, two on Rusthall and three on Tunbridge Wells Common, where Brighton Lake is the largest. Here can be found waterweeds such as Curly Water Thyme (*Lagarosiphon major*) and New Zealand Waterweed (*Crassula helmsii*). Both plants have been introduced into garden centres from abroad, sold to owners of garden ponds and when they spread too rapidly, discarded into local ponds and rivers. There are some native plants such as Broad Leaved Pondweed (*Potamogeton natans*) which floats on the water with dark oval leaves and a spike of tiny flowers in May. The Yellow Iris (*Iris pseudacorus*) which blooms in splendour in June, traditionally is the original fleur de lys, and Gipsywort (*Lycopus europaeus*), with its whorls of white flowers, follows later. Other ponds have some rather scarce specimens such as Water Milfoil (*Myriophyllum* spp.) with its delicate feathery leaves and Bogbean (*Menyanthes trifoliata*) whose conspicuous spikes of pink and white blossoms can be seen in June. Floating on the surface of the water can be seen Flote Grass (*Glyceria fluitans*), sometimes known as Water Grass, which is eagerly grazed by cattle on account of its succulent foliage. One of the loveliest sights on the larger marl pit pond at Rusthall in May are the flowers of the water buttercups Water Crowfoot (*Ranunculus aquatilis*) covering the whole area with masses of wide open white petals which give the illusion of snow. Later another spectacular plant can be seen at the edge in one corner, Purple Loosestrife (*Lythrum salicaria*), looking very striking and growing up to four feet high. Loosestrife is a literal translation of the Greek name for the plant which was believed to be 'so powerful that if placed on the yoke of incompatible oxen it will restrain their quarrelling'. As well as the ponds there are other wet places with water loving plants. One little area produces Ragged Robin (*Lychnis flos-cuculi*), bright pink with ragged petals, which makes a splendid band of colour along the edge of the tiny stream. With it grows another buttercup the Lesser Spearwort (*Ranunculus flammula*)

A History and Natural History

and two small white flowers, Bog Stitchwort (*Stellaria alsine*) and Marsh Bedstraw (*Galium palustre*), all common plants of watery places.

Drainage ditches are also damp places and here grows another lily, Ramsons (*Allium ursinum*), with umbels of long-stalked, white flowers and broad leaves which smell strongly of onions if trodden on. Nearby grows Himalayan Balsam (*Impatiens glandulifera*), which is relatively new in our flora. It was introduced from Asia in 1839 as a greenhouse annual and it had escaped to river banks by 1855. After that there is no mention of it in local or general floras until the 1940s when it appeared not only locally but along most of the rivers in the country. Jumping Jacks is one familiar name from the explosive method of its seed dispersal; another, Policemen's Helmet, is from the shape of the flower. On one patch of damp ground can be found the Common Spotted Orchid (*Dactylorhiza fuchsii*), whose numbers vary from year to year. Until 1970 another orchid was recorded Twayblade (*Listera ovata*); perhaps it will reappear. The orchids have a unique method of propagation involving a partnership with a fungus underground and although they produce a prodigious amount of very tiny seeds, it can take from five to fifteen years for them to germinate and come into flower, so it is very important that they are never picked. Near the orchids is the Common Yellow Sedge (*Carex demissa*), which is a typical plant of damp acid soils, but strangely very close by grow two species that are more usually found on chalk grassland, the first being Fairy Flax (*Linum catharticum*), a tiny slender annual only two to six inches high with small white flowers and threadlike stalks. At one time it was used as a purgative. The other is Quaking Grass (*Briza media*), a very distinctive grass with its green and purple spikelets hanging on slender stalks which shake in the wind and give rise to names such as Totter Grass and Dithery Docks.

Looking at postcards of the Commons at the turn of the nineteenth to twentieth centuries, it can be seen that they were very different from today: then there were fewer trees and large areas were covered with scrub, gorse, saplings, and rough grassland grazed by cattle and sheep. The change has taken place for various reasons: lack of management due to two world wars, and the advent of the motor car whose speed meant that the animals could no longer range freely. So grazing ended, the grass grew lusher, the saplings became full grown trees and the brambles spread. In spite of this there are still areas where heathland flora can be found, such as Heath Grass (*Danthonia decumbens*) and Mat Grass (*Nardus stricta*), a very typical grass of poor soil which just about holds on at one site. Flowers such as Heath Bedstraw (*Galium saxatile*) cover the grass with a carpet of tiny white flowers in June and Sheep's Sorrel (*Rumex acetosella*) gives a reddish brown colour to the ground on which it grows. In July, a dainty little blue flower grows on both Commons, the Harebell (*Campanula rotundifolia*), which was once a very common flower

Tunbridge Wells and Rusthall Commons

Common Dog Violet

Buckshorn Plantain

A History and Natural History

indeed, but unfortunately its numbers are falling, perhaps due to encroaching trees. Although it looks very fragile it is quite hardy but it does need plenty of light. Later in the year the Heather or Ling (*Calluna vulgaris*) shows its purple spikes which are very attractive to butterflies and bees. This is a plant that has spread since the new management, but very little Bell Heather (*Erica cinerea*) survives, growing along the Terrace Walk. The best known heathland plant is probably Gorse (*Ulex europaeus*) otherwise known as Furze or Whin. Of the pea family, its almond scented, bright yellow flowers can be found at any month of the year. Although it is extremely spiny it has been used for almost everything from feeding cattle, providing fuel for bakers' ovens, to use as brushes for chimney sweeps. Because of the sandy nature of the soil quite a few flowers usually associated with the coast are here. Storksbill (*Erodium circutarium*), with either pink or white petals, is a good example of the geranium family which comes out in May and lasts until the frosts start. The name Storksbill is from the shape of the seedhead said to resemble the bird's bill. Buckshorn Plantain (*Plantago coronopus*) is another mainly coastal plant with its attractive rosette of leaves close to the ground which look like the antlers of a deer. It has a spike of minute brownish flowers. On the edge of the cricket pitch in Tunbridge Wells and near Toad Rock in Rusthall, another sand loving plant grows: Birdsfoot (*Ornithopus perpusillus*) a very small peaflower which is rather infrequent in Kent but has been growing here at least since 1871 when Richard Deakin mentioned it in his book *The Flowering Plants of Tunbridge Wells*. Its flowers are so minute that to appreciate them properly it is best to look at them with a lens or magnifying glass, when the beautiful red-veined, very pale yellow flowers can be properly appreciated. Docks are plants which do not raise much interest. There are at least four found here: Broad Dock (*Rumex obtusifolius*), Wood Dock (*Rumex sanguineus*) and Curled Dock (*Rumex crispus*) are common species, but one, Fiddle Dock (*Rumex pulcher)*, is rarely seen away from the coast. It is smaller, only growing to about one foot high, with the lower leaves waisted or fiddle shaped, hence its name. Flowers of the Fiddle Dock grow in whorls on long stiff branches which spread at right angles, making it easy to distinguish from other docks which produce a spike of flowers. This is another plant recorded by Richard Deakin (1871).

As the year progresses the flora alters. The grasses now include Red Fescue (*Festuca rubra*), Rough Meadow Grass (*Poa trivialis*), Yorkshire Fog (*Holcus lanatus*) and later, Bent Grass (*Agrostis* spp.). The spring flowers such as Cow Parsley and Pignut have died off but two different umbellifers have replaced them and one, Hogweed (*Heracleum sphondylium*), is a stout, coarse, hairy biennial with hollow stems found on the edge of the grassland. As its name implies it was used as a fodder plant for pigs. It can grow up to

Tunbridge Wells and Rusthall Commons

five feet high but must not be mistaken for the Giant Hogweed (*Heracleum mantegazzianum*) which can grow up to ten feet high with the umbels up to four feet across and the main stalk two to four inches wide. A few years ago it appeared on the Common by Major York's Road and was probably bird sown. It is usually found in damp places near rivers. The other later umbellifer is Hedge Parsley (*Torilis japonica*), which is much daintier than the Hogweed, and although it is not as common as Cow Parsley, it is still plentiful along the roadside. It has solid stems and the flowers grow in long stalked umbels, either pink or white. Its seedheads are egg-shaped with hooked bristles. An attractive member of the willow-herb family, flowering in July, whose spikes of bright pink blossoms are very noticeable, is Rosebay (*Chamaenerion angustifolium*), known as Fireweed in America as it springs up after forest fires. It is a native plant but until the twentieth century was very uncommon and found only in damp woods. In the late nineteenth century the botanists considered it rare in the wild but common in gardens; the Reverend Johns, the author of *Flowers of the Field* (1890) advised owners of small gardens 'not to plant it as its rhizomes creep extensively and are very difficult to eradicate'. With the felling of many trees in both world wars, forest fires became more frequent and the plant spread. Once it is established it is easy to see why as each plant can produce some thirty thousand seeds and their plumes of long silky hairs are easily blown to great distances. On both Commons from June onwards can be seen a very handsome plant growing from two to three feet high with a head of bright yellow flowers. It is Common Ragwort (*Senecio jacobaea*), a composite. Unfortunately, it is a troublesome weed on farmland and is so poisonous to horses and cattle that it is on the list of noxious weeds that by law have to be kept under control, but it is the food plant of the yellow and black striped caterpillars of the Cinnabar moth and these are very efficient in keeping the weeds in check. Nevertheless it is an attractive plant to look at.

One group that has not been mentioned is the Polypodiaceae or ferns. Everyone knows the Bracken (*Pteridium aquilinum*), which can be recognized by its stalks which arise at intervals from a creeping rootstock. These branch into fronds some way from the ground. The fronds of other ferns such as the Male Fern (*Dryopteris filix-mas*) and Buckler Fern (*Dryopteris dilatata*) grow from the base of the rootstocks and very fascinating they look in May as they uncurl, resembling bishop's croziers. Not so common is the Hard Fern (*Blechnum spicant*) with its stiff, leathery fronds. These are barren, but in summer, fertile ones that are taller, thinner and more upright, bear spore cases. After the spores have been dispersed the fronds die but the sterile ones remain in a dark green rosette throughout the winter. On Rusthall Common is a very special fern, the Royal Fern (*Osmunda regalis*) which is now only plentiful in western Ireland. It was once quite common, but since the Victorian craze for

A History and Natural History

fern collecting depleted it over most of the country, it is now quite scarce. It looks rather like a flowering plant but it is the central fronds that are covered with spores that give the appearance of a spike of brown flowers. A little fern, Adder's Tongue (*Ophioglossum vulgatum*), once grew on Tunbridge Wells Common, but with improvements to paths and a lowering of the water table levels it has not been seen since 1973.

Trees have been referred to earlier, especially those with showy blossom, but later all the trees have the beauty of autumn colours. The Oak (*Quercus robur*) is one of the best known, and before the industrial revolution was the major provider for the making of ships and houses. Its flowers are insignificant but all know its fruit, the acorns. Its leaves are very easy to recognize and they are the latest to turn colour in November. Beeches (*Fagus sylvatica*) are fewer in number. Again the flowers tend to be overlooked, and it produces edible fruits, beech nuts or mast, but it is the magnificent golden leaves in the autumn that are outstanding. Probably the most numerous tree is the Silver Birch (*Betula pendula*) with paper-white bark and thin drooping branches with catkins and yellow leaves in October. A graceful tree is the Ash (*Fraxinus excelsior*); its leaves are the latest to appear in the spring and they fall early. The Sycamore (*Acer pseudoplatanus*) is not a native but came from Europe in the fifteenth century. It grows very quickly and soon colonizes an area where the seeds fall. Its dull green leaves often have large black spots on them caused by a fungus. Rowan or Mountain Ash (*Sorbus aucuparia*) has small white flowers in May which are followed by clusters of bright red berries. These are sour but pungent and often used for wine making. Various willows including Pussy Willow (*Salix caprea*) and Crack Willow (*Salix fragilis*) occur, but another one that is not a tree but a small undershrub is Creeping Willow (*Salix repens*) and it has the distinction of being the only recorded specimen in Kent.

As the end of the year approaches the evergreens become more noticeable. A few conifers such as the Yew (*Taxus baccata*) are to be found, mostly in one section of Tunbridge Wells Common, and are quite young trees. There are at least two Scots Pine (*Pinus sylvestris*), one fine specimen was growing near Fir Tree Pond until very recently. One very old Larch (*Larix decidua*) is still to be seen on Rusthall Common. Before the 1987 storm there was another growing off Castle Road which was felled on that night. It remained horizontal for some time after and even produced new leaves and cones before it was removed. Although not a conifer, the Holly (*Ilex aquifolium*) shows its shiny, evergreen, prickly leaves in many places. Holly trees are either male or female and on the Commons they are predominantly male which means that the familiar red berries only occur occasionally. Finally the Ivy (*Hedera helix*) is the last plant to flower in September with its clusters of small green flowers

Tunbridge Wells and Rusthall Commons

which develop into black berries early in the year.

There are over three hundred plants recorded on the Commons and these are just some of them to prove that whatever the time of year, the flora has something of interest and delight.

Flowerless Plants

Although flowering plants and ferns are generally the most conspicuous, they form only part of the flora of the Commons. While the flowering plants reproduce through pollination and the production of seeds, these so-called flowerless plants propagate themselves by means of spores, which lack the food reserves held in the seeds of higher plants. The bryophytes, which comprise the mosses and the closely related liverworts, are well represented on the Commons and are surprisingly varied in form when examined closely. Bryophytes rely on moist habitats, such as the shaded parts of the various rock formations. Since the sandstone outcrops here and elsewhere in the Weald provide a habitat unique in south-east England, the bryophyte flora of the Commons includes a number of species more characteristic of the west and north of Britain. Many mosses, such as the common *Ceratodon purpureum, Funaria hygrometrica* and *Pohlia nutans*, bear their spore capsules on long slender bright reddish stalks. Characteristic heathland mosses include the whitish green *Hypnum jutlandicum* and three members of the genus *Polytrichum* (*P. formosum, P. juniperinum and P. piliferum*), whose spore capsules have distinctive hairy caps. Liverworts on the Commons range from broad lobed forms like the common *Marchantia polymorpha* to more moss-like leafy types such as the heathland species *Lophozia ventricosa* and *Nardia scalaris*.

Lichens differ from bryophytes in their ability to survive and flourish in dry, exposed situations. They are composite plants, formed from a fungus and an alga in symbiosis. The fungus provides the lichen's protective outer structure, while the alga produces food by photosynthesis. On the Commons, as elsewhere, a wide variety of species may be found growing not only on rocks and trees, but also on man-made structures such as posts and benches. Some are brightly coloured, like the familiar orange-yellow *Xanthoria parietina* and its less common relative *X. calcicola*. Although many lichens form flat crusts on stone or wood, others have a looser branching structure, for example the grey-green *Evernia prunastri* and *Ramalina farinacea*, which grow on trees. Among the characteristically heathland lichens of the Commons are several species of the distinctive upright genus *Cladonia* (some being popularly known as cup or reindeer mosses), including *C. chlorophaea* and *C. coccifera*, both with grey-green cups but the latter with bright red spore-producing structures on the rims, and *C. rangiformis* which has a bushy many-

A History and Natural History

Crab apple

Ragwort.

Tunbridge Wells and Rusthall Commons

Coral Root

Hogweed

Ragged Robin

Rosebay

A History and Natural History

Rusthall Common photographed by George Glanville, from his album of 1884

Watercolour by Alfred Robert Quinton of the Common from Mount Ephraim, *c.*1912

Tunbridge Wells and Rusthall Commons

Mount Edgcumbe Rocks during clearing in the winter of 1994-5

Mount Edgcumbe Rocks after clearing

Bracken Cottage Pond after restoration

Mount Edgcumbe Rocks, partially cleared

A History and Natural History

branched form. As with bryophytes, a number of predominantly northern and western lichens occur, such as *Baeomyces rufus*, *Ochrolechia androgyna* and *Lecanora gangaleoides*.

Unlike other plants, fungi lack the green pigment chlorophyll and cannot generate food through the action of sunlight: they rely on absorbing nourishment from living plants, dead wood, or organic matter in the soil. The only part of a fungus that is normally seen is the short-lived fruiting body which produces the spores. Although some species of fungi can be found at any time of year, autumn is the season when most make themselves visible, and a walk over the Commons at this time can produce an extensive list of species. Among the more conspicuous and brightly coloured are the Fly Agaric (*Amanita muscaria*), the most familiar toadstool with its white-spotted scarlet cap, the bright yellow Sulphur Tuft (*Hypholoma fasciculare*), which grows in clusters, and the beautiful purple Amethyst Deceiver (*Laccaria amethystea*). Many members of the genus *Russula*, an extensive group with a pronounced family resemblance, exhibit striking colours on their caps, for example the deep purple *R. atropurpurea*, the green *R. aeruginea* and the bright red *R. sanguinea*. The genus *Boletus*, containing some large and conspicuous species with characteristic stout stems, is also well represented on the Commons, as are the ink-caps of the genus *Coprinus*. The blue-green *Chlorosplenium aeruginascens is* a small but interesting fungus growing on fallen timber, which itself becomes stained blue-green; the coloured wood was once much sought after by the manufacturers of Tunbridge ware. Some of the smaller puff-balls occur on the Commons, including *Lycoperdon perlatum* and *L. pyriforme*, as does the Common Earth-ball (*Scleroderma citrinum*) and some of its relatives. The bracket fungi, projecting conspicuously from the trunks of trees, are represented by such species as the Artist's Fungus (*Ganoderma applanatum*), the Razor-strop Fungus (*Piptoporus betulinus*) and the Giant Polypore (*Meripilus giganteus*).

I.C.B.

Tunbridge Wells and Rusthall Commons

MANAGEMENT OF THE COMMONS
Steve Budden

Until the beginning of the twentieth century, the Commons were dominated by heathland with comparatively few trees except those deliberately planted to commemorate events of importance to the town such as royal visits. It was a very different landscape than that which we see today, open views over scrubby vegetation with large amounts of gorse, bare sandy patches and extensive areas of grasses and heather. Dotted around the landscape would have been the sheep and cattle belonging to those with the Rights of Common that allowed them to graze their animals there. This view would probably have remained essentially unchanged for at least two thousand years and possibly more. It is important to understand the reasons for the dramatic change into the mainly wooded landscape that we see today in order to appreciate the Commons Conservators' plans for the future management of the Commons.

Heathland is defined by the *Oxford English Dictionary* as 'open uncultivated ground; a bare, more or less flat tract of land, naturally covered with low herbage and dwarf shrubs, especially heather and ling'. This is only half correct. Heathland is indeed dominated by a characteristic group of plants – dwarf shrubs, which are a constant feature of heathlands. But heathlands are a far from natural habitat, owing their existence to human activities over many centuries.

Heathland arises primarily in areas where the underlying rock strata result in the formation of poor, acidic and often sandy soils, such as occur on Tunbridge Wells Common. Such soils drain very freely and as a result there is a general downward movement of materials within them. Fine clay and humus particles are washed through by the movement of water and elements such as calcium, magnesium, sodium and potassium are leached by chemical processes in which they are replaced by hydrogen ions causing an acidification of the upper soil layers. In areas where rainfall is constantly higher than water loss through transpiration of plants and evaporation, the leaching process alone can be enough both to cause and maintain a heathland ecology. In southern England however this is not the case and another element is needed to bring about this state of affairs – human influence.

As long ago as the Iron Age, people had cleared the forest cover extensively. This was carried out to clear land for agriculture and to provide fuel and materials. Those areas with a rich soil structure became arable land, but those areas with poor, thin soils did not prove so useful. Many of the poorer areas were given over to grazing and the action of the animals prevented trees regenerating and on the poorest, most acidic soils, the leaching process

A History and Natural History

previously described could take place without any trees to pull the nutrients back up from the depths of the soil and recycle them into the upper layers through the decay of fallen leaves. By the sixth or seventh century, the feudal lifestyle was underway. Many of these marginal, infertile areas of land became the mainstay of those at the bottom of society who, through the generosity of their overlords, were sometimes given rights to make use of them. These usually consisted of the right to graze a certain number of beasts, but sometimes there were additional rights to collect bracken and heather for bedding and fodder. The desperate attempts of too many people trying to scrape a living from these 'common areas' of course merely depleted the soils even further, creating regions where only the toughest of species such as heather and gorse could survive. By at least the Middle Ages heathland was a very widespread habitat over much of southern Britain. Remnants can still be seen stretching from Sussex with Ashdown Forest, across Surrey with Bagshot Heath, across the Hardy County of Dorset and down across Dartmoor and Exmoor to the Lizard.

With such an extensive habitat existing over many centuries, inevitably plant and animal communities evolved to exploit this ecological niche. The most abundant and conspicuous shrubby species are Common Heather or Ling, Cross-leafed Heather, Bell Heather and Gorse. Lichens such as Reindeer Moss and Devil's Matches carpet the ground between the heather bushes. Although grasses are not usually the dominant plants, many species are found scattered throughout heathland such as Sheep's Fescue, Wavy Hair-grass, Common Bent and, in the wetter areas, Purple Moor Grass. Other typical herbaceous plants include Sheep's Sorrel, Heath Bedstraw, Tormentil and Slender St John's Wort. Most of these plants are typical of dry heath and although some are also found in wetter areas, there are species such as the Marsh Gentian, Round-leafed Sundew and Cotton Grass, which are confined to the damper areas. All six species of reptile found in Britain occur on heathlands, Adders, Grass Snakes, Smooth Snakes, Common Lizards, Sand Lizards and Slow Worms. All three species of newt, Great Crested, Smooth and, most commonly, Palmate; as well as toads, common frogs and Natterjack toads make use of heathland; the Natterjack toad is exclusive to heathland. British heathlands are rich in invertebrates. Many species favour the warm, sunny conditions found on south facing slopes and use patches of exposed, sandy soil as nesting sites. About half the species of dragonfly that occur in this country can be found on heathland and although there are no butterflies confined exclusively to heathland, it is still a vitally important habitat to them. Grasshoppers are widespread on heathland as are many species of solitary bees and wasps. It is also a key habitat for spiders as can be seen in the numbers of dew-soaked webs visible on gorse and heather bushes in the early

Tunbridge Wells and Rusthall Commons

View towards Mount Edgcumbe from above Gibraltar, *c.*1890

A similar view, March 2000

A History and Natural History

morning. A few of Britain's rarer birds need large, undisturbed areas of heath to hunt over and raise their young. The Red-backed Shrike and the Dartford Warbler rely on heathland habitats, and the Hobby, a rare bird of prey, and the Nightjar, an insect eater, are also to be found there. Many of these characteristic heathland species still survive on Tunbridge Wells and Rusthall Commons, and some now absent are known to have occurred there in the past.

By the mid-nineteenth century, the heathland lifestyle was in decline. Social and technological changes brought about by the industrial revolution meant that commons became less important. As many of those who used the commons moved away to towns and cities to work in the new factories, the numbers of animals grazing the heath declined as did the collection of bracken and heather. Improved ploughs and other agricultural equipment, plus the advent of artificial fertilizers, meant that areas of land previously considered marginal could now be brought into production. The immense loss of the young men of the country in the First World War also had its effect on reducing the heathland lifestyle. This trend continued with the drive for intensive agricultural production. Grants and subsidies for bringing land into both farming and forestry have accelerated habitat loss. According to figures issued by the Nature Conservancy Council, lowland heath has declined in area from 353,828 acres in 1830, to 97,442 acres in 1980; an overall loss of 72% (Webb 1986).

The heathland on Tunbridge Wells and Rusthall Commons declined along with heathland over the rest of southern England, but it avoided the fate of being taken into agricultural production, or, as would have been more likely given its position in the town, being built on. The discovery of the chalybeate springs by Lord North in 1606 started a chain of events that led to our Commons becoming far more important as a leisure resource for the town than as a place for commoners to graze their animals. The Commons were a major attraction for the town throughout the eighteenth and nineteenth centuries. Those who followed the royal example of taking the health giving waters would spend part of their days walking the Commons, enjoying the views, and marvelling at the grandeur of the rock outcrops. In 1890, following the passing of the Tunbridge Wells Improvement Act, the control of the Commons passed to the Commons Conservators, an independent body of twelve, consisting of four representatives each from the Borough Council, the Manor of Rusthall, (who still own the freehold on the land), and the Freehold Tenants, (who own property within the Manor boundaries). The Act (whose provisions relating to the Commons were re-enacted in 1981) confirms the boundaries of the Commons, the powers of the Conservators to make by-laws and to regulate the use of the Commons, and lays out the formula under which the Borough Council pays for the management of the land in exchange for free, unlimited public access. The Act charges the Conservators with preventing loss or

Tunbridge Wells and Rusthall Commons

encroachment on to the Commons, and with managing the Commons for the benefit of the residents of and visitors to the town. There is a certain irony that the future of the Commons was secured at just the time when social factors were ensuring the end of the very habitat for which it was so prized. Grazing of sheep and cattle on the Commons declined after the First Word War and ceased altogether sometime between 1928 and 1945. The widespread military use of the Commons in World War II for anti-aircraft gun and searchlight emplacements may have been the final factor to have stopped the grazing. Certainly, the mass removal of gorse to reduce fire risk did much to allow the fast colonising scrub to dominate the Commons. By the 1960s almost all of the heath and grassland had been swallowed up by the scrub and most of the rock outcrops were lost under a tide of trees, while the ponds that had been vital to grazing animals silted up and became overgrown. Many of the plants and animals that had thrived on the Commons also went into decline as their favoured habitat vanished. The fragility of the man-made heathland habitat could not be more clearly shown. Having lasted for at least 2000 years under its traditional management regime, it was lost in less than 100 years after that regime ceased. Little notice was taken of this change in the landscape of the town until the great storms of 1987 and 1990 caused landowners all over southern England to reassess their management. In 1990 the Conservators wisely took the decision to call in the Kent Trust for Nature Conservation to survey the Commons and to prepare a strategy for their future management. The Conservators adopted the resulting management plan in 1992.

The Commons Management Strategy

The recommendations of the plan can be summarized under six management objectives:

Objective 1 – To maintain and enhance the areas of heathland and acid grassland

This objective was considered the most urgent in view of the previously described loss of this habitat nationally. A countywide scheme is now underway to regenerate pockets of heathland to act as stepping stones to link remaining areas, if managed appropriately. Tunbridge Wells and Rusthall Commons would be a valuable part of this network. Without active management the areas of heather and grass would not survive. The ideal form of management would be to reintroduce grazing animals to the Commons. However, this was not considered viable in view of the Commons' position, the number and busyness of the roads crossing them and the numbers of dog owners who regularly exercise their pets there. The alternative adopted by the Conservators is to use mechanical means such as cutting and mowing to achieve the desired effect. In many areas of the Commons grasslands now

A History and Natural History

View across Tunbridge Wells Common towards Mount Ephraim, *c.*1905

A similar view, March 2000

Tunbridge Wells and Rusthall Commons

remain uncut until July to allow the wild-flowers within the sward to bloom and set seed, the resultant hay crop being removed to maintain low soil nutrient levels. Some areas of acid grassland have been much improved by being cut with a reciprocating cutter once a year, again with the cuttings removed to keep down nutrient levels and starve out the coarser species. New areas of heather are emerging as scrub and trees have been removed from parts of the Commons allowing dormant grass and heather seeds to germinate. Areas of bracken are being reduced by a regime of regular cutting or crushing and again heathland plants are emerging on these areas. In a new experiment, the Conservators have cleared all remaining vegetation and scraped off the topsoil on two areas that had been badly damaged by fire. The resulting clearing has subsequently been sown with heather seed harvested on Ashdown Forest. It has been pleasing to discover some of our remaining population of Common Lizards as well as our snakes moving into these new areas. Hopefully population numbers will increase as the new habitats mature. Green Woodpeckers have been quick to exploit the potential of the new areas to feed on the rising invertebrate numbers, as have the predatory dragonflies and damselflies that are also on the increase due to the next management objective.

Objective 2 – To maintain and enhance the areas of open water

When the Commons were being actively grazed there were, of necessity, several ponds established to provide drinking water. By the time of the adoption of the management plan in 1992 the only remaining areas of open water on the Commons were Brighton Lake on Tunbridge Wells Common and one of the ponds at the Marl Pits on Rusthall Common, which was quickly becoming silted-up. The Conservators have now restored Fir Tree Pond and Bracken Cottage Pond on Tunbridge Wells Common and deepened the surviving marlpit pond as well as partially restoring a second marlpit. This has resulted in not only increased numbers of dragonflies as previously mentioned, but has also greatly benefited the amphibian population. All of the ponds hold good numbers of frogs and toads, as well as both Smooth and Palmate Newts. The larger marlpit pond has a breeding population of the now rare Great Crested Newt. Grass Snakes regularly use all of the ponds to hunt frogs. It is hoped to continue opening up more of the old grazing ponds in the future.

Objective 3 – To manage appropriately existing areas of secondary woodland and scrub

Because of its comparatively recent succession, the secondary woodland that has colonized the area since the loss of grazing is less important in the management plan's conservation objectives. By the 1990s the Commons had a small amount of species-rich grassland and heathland, and a large amount

A History and Natural History

of species-poor woodland. As has already been explained, it has been necessary to remove some woodland and scrub to regenerate some of the more sensitive habitats. However, it is the intention of the Conservators to retain much of the woodland, partly to create as diverse a habitat as possible, and partly to act as a shield against traffic noise and fumes. The woodland that remains will be enhanced where appropriate by the creation and widening of paths and glades to increase the valuable woodland edge habitat as well as allowing greater access to human users of the Commons and acting as firebreaks to minimize potential damage. Some woodland will be thinned, concentrating on taking out non-native species such as sycamore, and replanting will take place with native species. Some areas will remain in the almost impenetrable state left by the storms.

Objective 4 – To recreate visual aspects of historic interest such as the vistas and the rock outcrops

This is probably the most difficult objective to achieve. The views and vistas that the Commons were so famous for in their past, have now almost all been lost. Whilst it would be perfectly possible to remove the trees that now obscure the views, all this would achieve in most cases would be to open up a view of busy roads or modern developments. Great care will be needed in deciding how much of this objective is appropriate. The rock outcrops are slightly less difficult to bring back, but in areas such as Happy Valley on Rusthall Common, large numbers of trees have had to be removed to re-expose the rock. Mount Edgcumbe Rocks on Tunbridge Wells Common are slowly being revealed again, and in the Denny Bottom area, Toad Rock and Bulls Hollow are being gradually opened up. This last area was scheduled as a geological Site of Special Scientific Interest by English Nature in 1992.

Objective 5 – To safeguard all notable species

There are several rare or locally rare species of plants on the Commons, the most notable being Coral Root, which occurs on both Commons. Special care is required when carrying out work in these areas to minimize disturbance. It is obviously more difficult to safeguard insects and birds. However, it is hoped that by following sensible guidelines, e.g, undertaking woodland work only during the winter to avoid disturbance during the nesting season, species will be able to move throughout the site when work is ongoing in certain areas.

Objective 6 – To promote tourism and improve visitor access and facilities on the Commons

At present, the Commons are, in practice, only accessible to local residents who are aware of their existence. To the visitor to the town, the Commons' interest, diversity and size are not at all apparent. It is always a difficult balance when managing areas of public land for wildlife benefit. Attracting

Tunbridge Wells and Rusthall Commons

too many visitors to a site can destroy the very peace and diversity that we are struggling to re-create. On the other side of the coin, the more we attract visitors to the Commons and therefore the town, the safer will be the future of the Commons in their present form. To capitalize on this asset, paths have been widened and the access points onto the Commons are being made easier as, in conjunction with the Tunbridge Wells Borough Council highways department, we are gradually improving road crossing and signage. For all users of the Commons the wider paths and improved views make the area feel safer, and as use of the Commons increases, that sense of personal security should increase. A leaflet detailing walks on both Commons is now available from the tourist information centre at the Pantiles and it is hoped over the next few years to provide interpretative signs to provide more information for visitors. A programme of improvements to surfaced paths across the Commons is underway and an all-ability trail is now in place in the area around the Wellington Rocks. Reproductions of the Victorian cast iron seats are gradually replacing the unsightly concrete ones that were installed in the period after the last war.

The issue of parking on the roads crossing the Commons is proving a very difficult one to resolve and the constantly rising number of cars in use mean that this problem is not going to lessen in the foreseeable future. There are many such issues – from illegal use of motorcycles to proposals for underground car parks, and from vandalism to attempted encroachment – that will continue to need the vigilance of the Conservators in the years ahead. However, it is to be hoped that the management criteria outlined here will continue to enhance these invaluable assets to the town.

A History and Natural History

Fir Tree Pond and Major York's Road, *c.*1905

A similar view, March 2000

Tunbridge Wells and Rusthall Commons

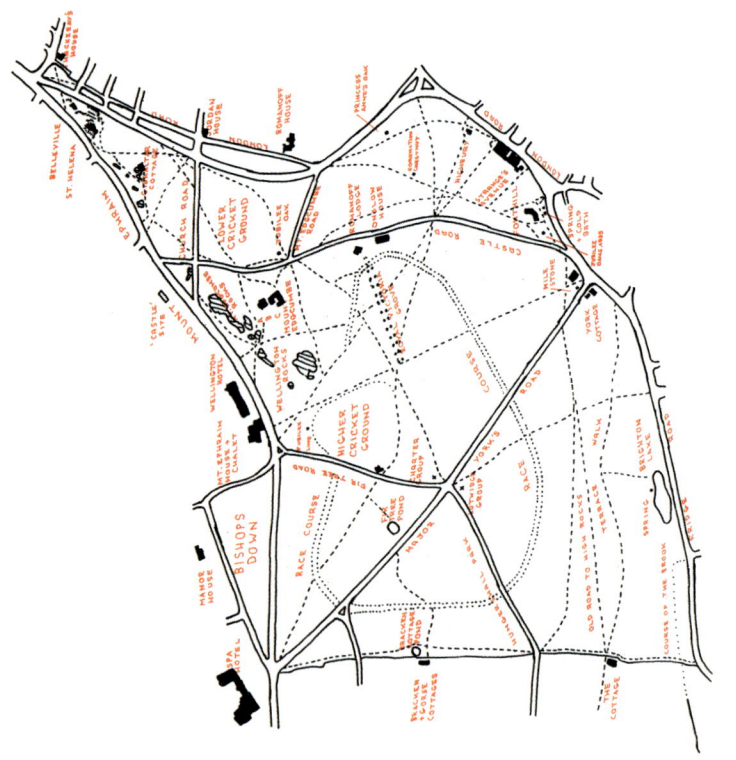

Sketch map of Tunbridge Wells Common

A History and Natural History

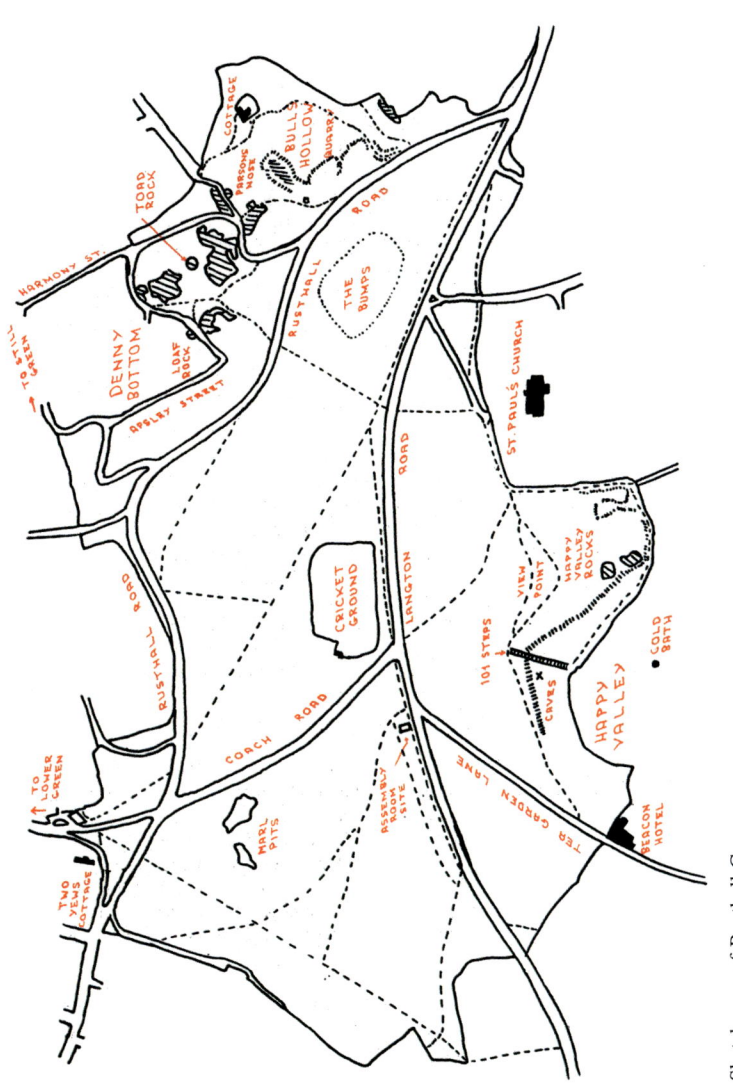

Sketch map of Rusthall Common

Tunbridge Wells and Rusthall Commons

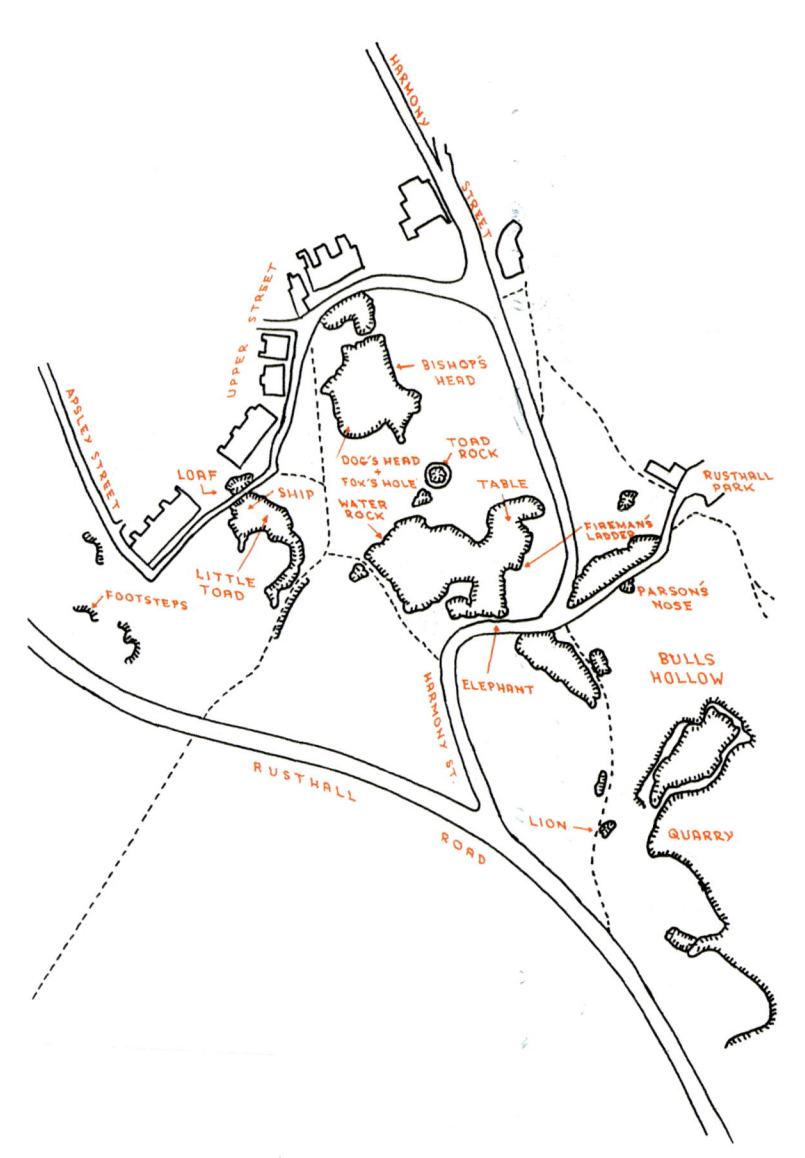

Sketch map of Denny Bottom

A History and Natural History

A TOUR OF THE COMMONS
Ian Beavis

TUNBRIDGE WELLS COMMON
beginning at the north-eastern corner

THACKERAY'S HOUSE – An early lodging house of the late seventeenth century, whose true name is Rock Villa. The novelist William Thackeray lodged here in 1860. He greatly enjoyed his walks over the Common, which he describes in his *Roundabout Papers*.

BELLEVILLE – Built probably about 1840 on the site of an earlier cottage shown on Bowra's map of 1738. Thackeray describes a house on the Common near Rock Villa in which he stayed as a child in 1823. This building has been identified with Belleville but was more likely Gibraltar, the only one of the three rock-built cottages at the apex of the Common known to have been used as a lodging house at that date.

SAINT HELENA – Built between 1828 and 1838 on the floor of a small stone quarry and used in early times as a lodging house. It replaced an earlier and much smaller cottage shown on Bowra's map of 1738 and illustrated in a number of eighteenth and nineteenth-century illustrations along with a second small structure to the north, on the other side of the rock. At the foot of the rocks a manhole cover marks the entrance to caves excavated for sand and open to the road until its level was raised in a controversial road levelling scheme carried out by the local Turnpike Trust in 1833. Residents complained that the loss of the caves spoiled the picturesque and much illustrated first view of the town which visitors saw as they travelled in from London. The caves were reopened at the outbreak of World War II to serve as air raid shelters.

GIBRALTAR COTTAGE – Built as a lodging house between 1814 and 1824 on the site of an earlier and smaller cottage of the same name. It was occupied by members of the Tunbridge ware making family of Burrows from the 1820s to *c*.1845. Having fallen into decay, it was restored and altered in 1970-71. The name is an allusion to the rocks on which the cottage stands; in the past Gibraltar has been used as a general term for the rocky eastern apex of the Common. Until the mid-nineteenth century, a pond known as Parson's Pond existed below the cottage alongside London Road.

JORDAN HOUSE – Premises occupied in the first half of the nineteenth

Tunbridge Wells and Rusthall Commons

century by Tunbridge ware makers Humphrey Burrows Senior and Junior. Their factory and show room was patronized by Princess Victoria, as is commemorated on a well-known print.

LOWER CRICKET GROUND – First used as a cricket pitch in the 1850s by the pupils of Romanoff House School. From 1860 it was the site of an annual bonfire on 5 November, and it was regularly used as a venue for civic celebrations of coronations and jubilees. It was levelled and railed in 1885-6. There was a Territorial Army encampment here in 1914. The original railings, along with those of the Higher Cricket Ground, were taken for the war effort in 1942.

JUBILEE OAK – Planted in June 1887 by Mrs Stone Wigg, wife of the Chairman of the Local Board, to celebrate Queen Victoria's golden jubilee.

MOUNT EDGCUMBE ROAD – Traditionally known as Donkey Drive, from which animals were hired for riding. This pastime was introduced in 1801, and enjoyed by Princess Victoria in the early 1830s, continuing into late Victorian times. The avenue of flowering cherries (King's Avenue) was planted in March 1937 for the coronation of George VI. The contemporary King's Grove, a circle of scarlet chestnuts between Mount Edgcumbe and Victoria Grove, did not flourish and the trees, described twenty years later as 'small and stunted', became obscured by the later growth of saplings.

MOUNT EDGCUMBE ROCKS – Well-known in Victorian and Edwardian times and a popular vantage point for views across the town. They were known to children of the mid-twentieth century as the Devil's Dyke. A pond at the foot of the rocks was filled in in 1879. By the 1960s the open grassy space in front of the rocks had become overgrown by scrub which obscured them completely, but the area was cleared in 1994-5.

MOUNT EDGCUMBE – A hillock named after Emma, Dowager Countess of Mount Edgcumbe, who spent the summers of 1795-7 in the town. The group of three buildings here appear as early as Bowra's map of 1738. They were originally two lodging houses (Mount Edgcumbe [A], now a Hotel, and Ephraim Lodge [C]) and a private house (Mount Edgcumbe Cottage [B]). The Arctic explorer Sir William Parry stayed at what is now the hotel in 1839.

MOUNT EPHRAIM PROMENADE – Originally levelled as a turf walk on the northern edge of the Common in 1881, but later gravelled (1891) and

A History and Natural History

Donkey Boys on the Common. A photograph by Percy Lankester, c.1890.

Tunbridge Wells and Rusthall Commons

asphalted (1925). Just as in the early nineteenth century seaside resorts modelled themselves on the older spas, so in later times Tunbridge Wells adopted seaside terminology. Alongside the Promenade is one of the Common's surviving areas of acid grassland, an important wildlife habitat.

WELLINGTON HOTEL – Opened in 1875 by John Braby. Braby was an admirer of the Duke, whose wife stayed in the town on a number of occasions.

MOUNT EPHRAIM HOUSE – Charles II and Queen Katharine stayed here in 1663 while their court camped on the Common. The house served as the Assembly Room for the entertainment of visitors from 1665 to 1670. It was substantially altered in the 1840s, acquiring an extra storey and a new façade. Together with the Chalet, built in its grounds around 1800, it served as the Tunbridge ware manufactory of William Fenner from the 1790s, the business being subsequently taken over by Edmund Nye around 1840 and Thomas Barton in 1863. Manufacture continued until Barton's death in 1903. On the edge of the Common around the corner of the boundary wall is a row of seats: this area was traditionally noted as a sun trap and named the South of France.

WELLINGTON ROCKS – Named after the Wellington Hotel. In earlier times they were variously described as the High Rocks on Mount Ephraim, or as Castle Rock (either named after the nearby Castle Tavern, or because of the shape of the rocks' highest point). Early nineteenth-century guides report that 'small transparent pebbles are found on the paths of the Common, especially after rain. These crystals are called Tunbridge Wells Diamonds, and, cut and polished, form brilliant additions to the jewel-case'. Small rounded pebbles can still be seen here today embedded in the sandstone, and it is presumably the most attractive of these, eroded out of the rock, which were once collected.

JUBILEE LIME – Planted in March 1977 to commemorate Elizabeth II's silver jubilee.

HIGHER CRICKET GROUND – Although cricket was played on this site informally from the mid-eighteenth century, its status as an official ground dates from 1839 when the newly formed Tunbridge Wells Cricket Club was given permission to use and improve it. It was enlarged in 1859 and 1875. County matches were played here from 1845 to 1880, but they ceased due to the poor condition of the pitch which was regularly trampled by the public and grazing animals. On either side of the pavilion are flowering cherries planted in June 1953 to commemorate Elizabeth II's coronation. Around the

A History and Natural History

Tunbridge Wells. A view of Queen Anne's Grove. A steel engraving by H. Adlard after a drawing by George Shepherd, 1828

The Common Tunbridge Wells. A watercolour by John Preston Neale of the south-western corner of Tunbridge Wells Common looking toward Ropers Gate, 1847

Tunbridge Wells and Rusthall Commons

cricket ground, and elsewhere on the Common, can be seen a number of cast iron 'hawthorn' benches dating from the 1860s and restored in the early 1990s; subsequently many replicas of the originals have also been made and installed.

ROYAL VICTORIA GROVE – Planted in February 1835 as a double avenue to commemorate visits to the town by Princess Victoria with her mother the Duchess of Kent. Just to the north was the earlier Queen's Grove, planted for the coronation of Queen Anne in 1702 and replanted in 1811; this never did well and died out in the early 1850s. Victoria Grove was planned as three rows of sycamores, limes, and elms, but some trees had to be replaced in later years and often did not conform to the original plan. The elms succumbed to disease in 1972, and in 1992 the third row was replanted to celebrate the fortieth anniversary of Elizabeth II's accession. For a few years from 1911 a moveable bandstand was set up to the south. To the north of the Grove is a small patch of surviving heathland, a type of vegetation once much more widespread on the Common.

RACE COURSE – Appears on Bowra's map of 1738 and remained in use until 1851. Race meetings were held for two days each year, in August or September. The winning post, stand, and enclosure stood on the north side of the present Higher Cricket Ground. The Duchess of Kent and Princess Victoria attended in 1834. In 1845 residents petitioned for the suppression of the races on the grounds that they were a cause of drunkenness and riotous behaviour. After races ceased to be held, the course (apart from the section crossing the Cricket Ground) was preserved as a footpath and can still be followed today. Along the southern section, between Major York's Road and Hungershall Park, is a clearing where heathland restoration is in progress. Near the north west corner is the site (formerly marked by a plaque) of a thatched shelter destroyed by a flying bomb in 1944, with the death of an elderly resident. Hidden in the undergrowth north of the car park where the race course meets Fir Tree Road is the site of a small quarry.

CASTLE ROAD – Possibly named after the Castle Tavern, opened between 1665 and 1670, which stood on Mount Ephraim between the junctions with Church Road and Castle Road. The building, no longer extant, was converted to a lodging house in the mid-eighteenth century. An alternative theory is that the tavern was named after Castle Rock (now Wellington Rocks).

ROMANOFF LODGE – Built in 1852 by Thomas Allfree on the site of a late eighteenth-century cottage occupying, along with Castle Cottage, the site of old gravel or sand pits. Allfree was the proprietor of Romanoff House

A History and Natural History

Air raid shelter in the caves beneath St Helena. A drawing by E. Owen Jennings, April 1941

Tunbridge Wells, from the Race-Course. A wood engraving of *c.*1850

Tunbridge Wells and Rusthall Commons

School (occupying the building in London Road now known as Vale Towers), founded by him in the 1830s; the present Rose Hill School is in lineal descent. Allfree used the name Romanoff because he had been a tutor to the Russian royal family.

ONSLOW HOUSE – The original Onslow House was built in the early 1880s on the site of the late eighteenth-century Castle Cottage. As a condition of permission to build, an old sand pit on the opposite side of the road latterly used as a stonemason's yard was filled in and restored to the Common. Onslow House was replaced by the present row of houses in 1965.

CORONATION CHESTNUT – A red-flowered tree planted in December 1911 to commemorate the coronation of George V. The trees that now surround it have all grown up subsequently.

PRINCESS ANNE'S OAK – Overlooking London Road, between Mount Edgcumbe Road and the Vale Road corner, is an oak tree said to have been planted around 1700 to commemorate the several visits of the Princess (later Queen) to Tunbridge Wells between 1684 and 1698. The Victorian railings around the tree were restored in 1995, and a plaque affixed.

HIGHBURY – A $c.$1906 rebuilding of Exeter Villa, a late eighteenth or early nineteenth-century lodging house. In the vicinity of the house is one of the Common's surviving areas of acid grassland, characterized by the nest mounds of the Yellow Meadow Ant. Lizards are frequently to be seen here.

STRANGE'S AVENUE – Planted $c.$1810-20 by Edward Hilder Strange, proprietor of the Royal Kentish Hotel, as an ornamental avenue leading down to his front entrance. It consisted originally of some forty sycamores and chestnuts, but many trees have been replaced in subsequent years.

FONTHILL – The present Fonthill Pavilion (which since 1993 has functioned as a live music venue known as The Forum) was built in 1939 by the Borough Council to provide 'rest rooms and general conveniences' for locals and visitors enjoying the Common. It replaced a forge, coach builder's workshop, and attached cottage (Fonthill House) dating from 1833. An earlier forge on the site is shown on Bowra's map of 1738. This is said to be the site of the cottage occupied by Mrs Humphreys, who provided Lord North with a cup to drink from the chalybeate spring when he discovered it in 1606. The buildings on the edge of the Common east and west of Fonthill were from early times an untidy clutter of small cottages and rough working buildings: the present

A History and Natural History

unattractive structures are in lineal descent. The present garage is on the site of the Kentish Stables, then belonging to the Royal Kentish Hotel opposite.

COLD BATH AND SPRING – The Cold Bath was constructed around 1766, falling into disuse with the construction of Bath House in 1804. The well was sunk over a chalybeate spring about 1700. Both structures became buried in the early nineteenth century and were rediscovered during road works in 1971.

JUBILEE OAKS OF 1935 – Contemporary press accounts report that a pair of scarlet chestnuts were planted near Fonthill in May 1935 to celebrate George V's silver jubilee. It is presumed that the original trees did not survive and that the two oaks on the site today are replacements.

MILESTONE – This small pillar of local sandstone originally indicated thirty-six miles to London, but is now illegible. It dates from at least the early nineteenth century.

YORK COTTAGE – Built by George Mercer, a chaise driver, who in 1820 obtained permission from the Freeholders and the Lady of the Manor (Elizabeth Shorey) to enclose a small portion of the Common for the purpose. It is a survivor of a number of small cottages on the Commons, most of which were replaced by more substantial structures in Victorian times.

CHARTER GROUP – A group of limes planted by John Stone Wigg, the first mayor of Tunbridge Wells, to celebrate the granting of borough status to the town in February 1889.

LUTWIDGE GROUP – The pine tree on the corner is the most conspicuous survivor of five trees planted in November 1895 by the mayor elect, Major C.R. Fletcher Lutwidge, as part of a scheme promoted by the Tradesmen's Association by which individuals and organizations had subscribed around 150 trees. Trees planted on the opposite corner by the outgoing mayor, Sir David Lionel Salomons, succumbed to a gorse fire.

FIR TREE POND – A noted beauty spot in Victorian and Edwardian times, named from a pair of Scots pines (affectionately named Darby and Joan) with a seat around them which stood on top of the slope above. Having succumbed to old age, they were cut down in 1914 and replacements, still to be seen today, were planted. The pond is situated in a an extensive hollow described in 1957 as an 'old quarry'. The pond was restored in 1992.

Tunbridge Wells and Rusthall Commons

ERIDGE ROAD – Formerly known as Brighton Road, hence the name given to the lake situated beside it. As is the case generally on the perimeter of the Commons, the Common officially extends across the road and includes the strip of grass with trees on the other side.

BRIGHTON LAKE – Fed by a chalybeate spring (visible on the northern edge) and excavated in 1858 as part of a scheme instigated by William Law Pope, minister of King Charles' church, to provide work for the town's unemployed, wages being paid by public subscription. It was nicknamed Pope's Puddle or Pope's Folly. The official name relates to the fact that it stands on the road to Brighton. Today the pond is an important habitat for wildlife, including frogs, toads, newts, grass snakes, and dragonflies.

TERRACE WALK – Revd Pope's unemployed workers also created a 'greensward terrace walk' above the pond.

ROAD TO HIGH ROCKS – The path just to the north of the terrace walk is the eighteenth-century road to High Rocks, whose continuation past the Cottage is known as Cabbage Stalk Lane. There are traces of old excavations for sand or gravel on its northern side.

THE BROOK – The small stream which once marked the county boundary flowed beside what is now Cumberland Walk, behind the Lower Walk of the Pantiles, and along Eridge Road before crossing the corner of the Common below the Cottage, the footpath to which once crossed a small bridge. In 1853, following years of complaints that it had become an open sewer and was a hazard to public health, it was finally enclosed in a barrel drain at the expense of the Local Board, assisted by a contribution from the Earl of Abergavenny. It now emerges in the garden centre beyond the western boundary of the Common. Although local residents never dignified it with a name, it is in fact the beginning of the River Grom.

THE COTTAGE – An enlargement of the late seventeenth or early eighteenth-century Kentish Cottage, named from the long vanished farmhouse known as Kentish Villa a little to the north. It was the summer retreat from *c.*1850 of the Scottish preacher Dr John Cumming. In front of the Cottage are oaks probably planted around 1700 to mark the boundary of the Common. Other trees of similar age can be seen further along the path to the north.

GORSE AND BRACKEN COTTAGES – Built about 1912 on the site of the early Victorian Spring Bottom Cottage, also known as Shoebridge's Cottage after a laundress who lived there in the 1860s.

BRACKEN COTTAGE POND – A modern name for a survivor of several informal ponds scattered over the Commons up to the mid-nineteenth century and maintained as watering places for cattle and sheep. Most were filled in at various dates between 1850 and 1900. This pond was restored in 1992. It is fed by a spring via a small watercourse to the east.

BISHOPS DOWN – Triangular portion of the Common with adjacent houses which preserves the ancient name of the entire Common. There was formerly a pond here, but in 1865 it was filled in.

MANOR HOUSE – Not a true manor house, but a late seventeenth-century lodging house acquired along with other property at Bishops Down by George Kelley at the time when he purchased the Manor of Rusthall. In lodging house lists of around 1800 it appears as Mrs Shorey's Great House, after the then Lady of the Manor. The present name dates from *c.*1822.

SPA HOTEL – Built in 1764 by Sir George Kelley, Lord of the Manor, as Bishops Down Grove. It was purchased from his heirs by Major Martin Yorke of the East India Company (after whom the road is named) in 1772. Its life as a hotel dates from 1878, when, following enlargement, it was opened as the Bishops Down Grove Spa and Hydropathic Sanatorium. On the strip of the Common in front of the hotel is a drinking fountain erected in 1887 in memory of the Hon. Francis and Lady Georgina Molyneux. Francis Molyneux moved to Tunbridge Wells in 1853, living first at Gibraltar Cottage and subsequently building Earls Court (now Reliance House) on Mount Ephraim. He was a leading member of the Freeholders, as well as the Local Board. Nearby, a plaque indicates an oak planted in July 1954 to commemorate a summer school held by the Men of the Trees, an early environmental group, at the Hotel.

RUSTHALL COMMON

DENNY BOTTOM – The settlement of Denny Bottom was described by John Britton in 1832 as consisting of 'broken ground, pig-sties, rude cottages and small enclosures'. Apart from the Hobblies (built in 1569), no buildings survive from that period, but the present layout of the area, with small dwellings clustering close to the rocks, preserves something of its early character. Small scale quarrying and sand digging continued here much later than elsewhere on the Commons, a quarry along Apsley Street being in use as recently as

Tunbridge Wells and Rusthall Commons

1914. The Toad Rock Retreat, established around 1880 and subsequently enlarged, was largely destroyed by fire in 1998 and rebuilt in similar style.

TOAD ROCK – First popularized in a local guide in 1810, it is not named until the 1823 edition of Clifford's Tunbridge Wells guide. It was fenced and the base strengthened with masonry in 1881-2. The original railings were renovated during the winter of 1993-4. Before geologists were able to explain its origin, it aroused much speculation, including the idea that it was possibly man-made. Some nineteenth-century observers believed that it was 'the remains of an ancient sphinx', and as late as 1933 H.G. Wells referred to this idea in his novel *Christina Alberta's Father*. The Toad and other outcrops were probably eroded into their present forms during the last Ice Age. As a result of this geological history, the surrounding area was designated a geological Site of Special Scientific Interest in 1992.

DENNY BOTTOM ROCKS – In Victorian and Edwardian times visitors to the Toad were liable to be accosted by self-appointed guides who would offer to point out the names of many other rocks in the vicinity. The oldest names appear to be those of the Loaf, the Lion (mentioned in the 1850s) and the Parson's Nose (painted under this name by Charles Tattershall Dodd in the 1840s, but named the Old Man's Head on a sketch of 1824 and the Pulpit on Edwardian postcards). Martin and Row's guide *Tunbridge Wells of Today* (*c*.1897) provides the only substantial published list (said to be far from complete) but gives no clue to precise locations. As well as the three mentioned in earlier sources, they name the Little Toad, Elephant, Fox's Hole and Footsteps, located through oral tradition for the present map, as well as the still unlocated Bloodstain, Cradle and Pig's Head. The Bloodstain, known to other sources as the Bleeding Rock, is generally understood as a spot where dripping water left an iron stain, but no site fitting this description can be pointed out today. Another named rock, the Dog's Head, is illustrated in a late Victorian print. Edwardian sources mention, as well as some of the above, the Table, Camel, and Double Rock, of which only the former can be identified today. Other names on the present map have been preserved only by oral tradition

BULL'S HOLLOW – An early twentieth-century beauty spot frequently illustrated in town guides, first popularized when in 1905 the Conservators cleared it of undergrowth and provided seats. At the time it was noted that the rock surface there 'presents different colours of a rich and varied character', although this is not evident today. Bull's Hollow is the site of a quarry (disused by 1890), named after Robert Bull, a quarryman who worked there and built

A History and Natural History

a cottage in the early nineteenth century. The original cottage, occupied by several generations of the Bull family, was enlarged into its present form in the 1950s. There was a military rifle range here in 1918-19. The rocks of the quarry were first publicized as a site for climbers in 1936.

STILL GREEN – A detached portion of Rusthall Common which today resembles an appendage to Hurst Wood. It is named Steel Green on Bowra's map of 1738.

LOWER GREEN – Another early settlement like Denny Bottom, clustered around a small detached portion of the Common. The Green proper is now much reduced in size through road widening but originally boasted a spring and a pond. The pond was filled in in 1899.

TWO YEWS COTTAGE – One of the oldest surviving houses in Tunbridge Wells, dating from the mid to late fifteenth century. The main part of the house would have been an open hall prior to alterations around 1600. There is a nineteenth-century addition to the original building.

MARL PITS – The most notable relics of several excavations for marl on Rusthall Common are two depressions which by the 1870s had developed into ponds. A bowling green was established to the south in 1913, but in time the site proved unsatisfactory and no trace remains today. Today the ponds are notable habitats for amphibians. The larger of the two was restored early in 1993, with further work in 1996. In the latter year, efforts were made to restore the second pond, but owing to its small size this is likely to remain a seasonal pool. Marl was a generic term for various kinds of clay which, it was believed, could be employed as fertilizer to make poor local soils more suitable for agriculture. This practise was popularized locally by Gervase Markham in his *Inrichment of the Weald of Kent* (1683). The two ponds seen today are simply the lowest points of a much more extensive, although relatively shallow, excavation whose boundaries can be seen on older maps. Other marl pit sites, some of which are much deeper, can be found north of St Paul's Church, north and north-east of the Cricket Ground, and in the triangle between Tea Garden Lane and Langton Road.

COACH ROAD – A surviving section of a road which in the mid-nineteenth century continued beyond Langton Road to the corner of the Common where the road now known as the Midway begins, after which it continued south to meet High Rocks Lane. At the junction with Rusthall Road is a drinking fountain erected in 1887 in memory of Margaret Cunliffe of Nevill Park.

Tunbridge Wells and Rusthall Commons

ASSEMBLY ROOM SITE – A bramble filled pit marks the site of the first Assembly Room for the entertainment of the visitors to the Wells, built in 1655 when most still lodged at Rusthall. In 1665 this facility was transferred to Mount Ephraim House. A contemporary bowling green extended to the west.

RUSTHALL CRICKET GROUND – Levelled in 1885-6, replacing an earlier unsatisfactory site established in 1865 at the north-western corner of the Common. It was enlarged in 1906. The informal playing field to the east, known as 'the Bumps' was cleared in the 1950s and levelled in 1961.

ST PAUL'S CHURCH – Built 1849-50, with a north aisle added in 1864. Edwardian views show on the western side of the footpath between the church and Langton Road a now vanished pond within the bounds of the enormous marl pit marked on Bowra's 1738 map. The avenue leading up to the church was planted to commemorate the accession of George V in 1910.

BEACON HOTEL – Built in 1895 as Rusthall Beacon by Sir Walter Harris (later Lord Mayor of London) on the site of two cottages attached to the original Tea Gardens, opened *c.*1818, after which the road is named. Together with the Tea Gardens site, he bought part of Cold Bath Farm, the area known as Happy Valley. The estate was bought in 1907 by Colonel Edward Sydney St Barbe Sladen (mayor of Royal Tunbridge Wells 1910-12), who erected in the grounds a Burmese temple bell brought back by his father Sir Edward Sladen which was later placed in Calverley Grounds. From 1938 and through World War II, the house was used as a residential home for Jewish refugee children. The building became a hotel in 1950.

HAPPY VALLEY – One of the town's chief beauty spots in Victorian and Edwardian times. There are many pictures of that period showing what was said to be 'as beautiful a view as England affords' from the traditional viewpoint marked today by a clearing to the east of the Hundred and One Steps. Nowadays, due to obscuring trees, the best view can be obtained from the footpath between the Steps and the Beacon Hotel. The name was invented around 1870 (after the earthly paradise in Samuel Johnson's *The History of Rasselas*, 1759) for what are now the grounds of the Beacon Hotel, but were originally the pleasure grounds surrounding the Cold Bath of 1708.

HUNDRED AND ONE STEPS – Constructed to provide the main access to the Cold Bath of 1708 and therefore presumed to be contemporary with it.

A History and Natural History

They appear on Bowra's map of 1738. By 1840 they had become covered by turf, and were apparently not revealed to view again until early in the twentieth century. Some postcards following their rediscovery erroneously describe them as 'the Roman Steps', creating a local legend that has endured to the present day. Missing and damaged steps were replaced by old kerbstones in 1959.

HAPPY VALLEY CAVES – Sometimes described as Sweeps' Caves because they were once used as a dump for soot. Colbran's town guide of 1839 describes them as 'dormitories for gipsies etc.'. They were probably intended originally to shelter wooden seats and excavated at the time of development of the Cold Bath to provide viewpoints over the valley.

HAPPY VALLEY ROCKS – Mesolithic flint implements found here suggest these were used as camp sites by nomadic hunters of the period, as the cliffs at High Rocks are known to have been; they would have used the overhangs (much higher above ground level than we see them today) as shelters. Early local botanists knew them as the Cold Bath Rocks. The rock nearest to the path is known as the Cheesewring (i.e. cheese-press) Rock, on account of the narrow gap separating the isolated stack from the cliff behind. The stack was underpinned with masonry in 1932. In the post-war period, the rocks above the path became obscured by undergrowth, but they were cleared in the mid-1990s.

COLD BATH – Lying just over the boundary of the Common in the Beacon Hotel grounds, the bath was constructed in 1708. The yew trees which surround it today are relics of contemporary hedges. It is sometimes described as Queen Anne's Bath, as a result of an erroneous local legend that the Queen patronized it, although in fact she did not visit Tunbridge Wells after 1700. It was originally covered by an ornamental pavilion and surrounded by gardens with lakes, watercourses, and fountains, but by 1766 it had fallen into disuse. One of the ancillary buildings survived as a cottage into the twentieth century, but today there are no upstanding remains. The three lakes to the south are the only other visible features of the original pleasure grounds, having been restored in the second half of the nineteenth century and improved by Colonel Sladen in 1907-10. Sladen's planting and landscaping of the grounds was regarded by his contemporaries as a triumph of horticultural art, but they were sadly neglected after the death of his widow in 1936.

Tunbridge Wells and Rusthall Commons

BIBLIOGRAPHY

Allen, P. 1990. 'Wealden research – Ways ahead'. *Proceedings of the Geologists' Association* 100(4): 529-564.

Allen, P. 1998. 'Purbeck-Wealden (early Cretaceous) climates'. *Proceedings of the Geologists' Association* 109(3): 197-236.

Amsinck, P. 1810. *Tunbridge Wells, and its Neighbourhood, Illustrated by a Series of Etchings, and Historical Descriptions.* London: W. Miller and E.Lloyd.

Beavis, I.C. 1995. *The Butterflies of Tunbridge Wells and District.* Tunbridge Wells: Tunbridge Wells Museum and Art Gallery.

Berry, W. 1830. *Pedigrees of the Families in the County of Kent.* London: Gilbert & Piper.

Bristow, C.R., and R.A. Bazley. 1972. 'Geology of the country around Royal Tunbridge Wells'. *Memoirs of the Geological Survey of the United Kingdom* 303.

Britton, J. 1832. *Descriptive Sketches of Tunbridge Wells & the Calverley Estate.* London: Longman and Co.

Burr, T.B. 1766. *The History of Tunbridge Wells.* London.

Cleere, H., and D. Crossley. 1995. *The Iron Industry of the Weald.* 2nd ed. Cardiff: Merton Priory Press.

Clifford, J. 1818 et seq. *Clifford's Descriptive Guide of Tunbridge Wells.* Tunbridge Wells: J. Clifford.

Crowson, R.A. 1938. 'The metendosternite in Coleoptera: a comparative study'. *The Transactions of the Royal Entomological Society of London* 87: 397-416.

Crowson, R.A. 1946. 'The fossil insects of the Weald'. In Given, J.C.M. (ed.). *Royal Tunbridge Wells – Past and Present.* Tunbridge Wells: Courier.

Crowson, R.A. 1981. *The Biology of the Coleoptera.* London: Academic Press.

Dashwood, F. 1987. *The Dashwoods of West Wycombe.* London: Aurum.

Deakin, R. 1871. *The Flowering Plants of Tunbridge Wells & Neighbourhood.* Tunbridge Wells: Stidolph & Bellamy.

Falk, S. 1991. *A Review of the Scarce and Threatened Bees, Wasps and Ants of Great Britain.* Peterborough: Nature Conservancy Council.

Farthing, R. 1990. *Royal Tunbridge Wells – A Pictorial History.* Chichester: Phillimore & Co. Ltd. Notes and references are available in typescript at Tunbridge Wells Reference Library and CKS and on Kent Family History Society microfiche no. 1754.

Forster, T. 1842. *Flora Tonbrigensis.* London: Hamilton, Adams and Co.

A History and Natural History

Gallois, R.W., and F.H. Edmunds. 1965. *The Wealden District.* 4th ed. British Geological Survey.

Goulden, R.J. 1995. *Kent Town Guides 1763-1900.* London: The British Library.

Grigson, G.E.H. 1955. *The Englishman's Flora.* London: Phoenix House.

Hamilton, C.J. 1905. 'From the Stage to the Peerage'. *Womanhood* XIV No 79 June 1905.

Harland, W.B., R.L. Armstrong, A.V. Cox, L.E. Craig, A.G. Smith, and D.G. Smith. 1990. *A Geologic Time Scale 1989.* Cambridge: Cambridge University Press.

Harris, J. 1719. *The History of Kent in Five Parts.* London: D. Midwinter.

Hasted, E. 1797. *The History and Topographical Survey of the County of Kent.* 2nd edition. Canterbury: Simmons and Kirkby.

Hembrey, P. 1990. *The English Spa 1560-1815 A Social History.* London: The Athlone Press.

Jarzembowski, E.A. 1984. 'Early Cretaceous insects from southern England'. *Modern Geology* 9: 71-93, pls. 1-4.

Jarzembowski, E.A. 1987. 'Early Cretaceous insects from southern England'. PhD thesis, University of Reading, 421 pp.

Jarzembowski, E.A. 1990. 'A boring beetle from the Wealden of the Weald'. In: Boucot, A.J. *Evolutionary Paleobiology of Behavior and Coevolution.* Amsterdam: Elsevier. Pp. 373-6.

Jellis, S. 1985. *History of the Manor of Rusthall.* University of Kent Diploma Dissertation.

Johns, C.A. 1890. *Flowers of the Field.* London: SPCK.

Knipe, H.R. 1916. 'Palaeontology'. In: Knipe, H.R. (ed.) *Tunbridge Wells and Neighbourhood.* Tunbridge Wells: Pelton.

Laurentiaux, D. 1953. 'Classe des Insectes' In: Piveteau, J. (ed.) *Traité de Paléontologie,* 3. Paris: Masson.

Mabey, R. 1996. *Flora Britannica.* London: Sinclair-Stevenson.

MacClintock, D., and R.S.R. Fitter. 1955. *The Pocket Guide to Wild Flowers.* London: Collins.

McRae, S.G., and C.P. Burnham. 1976. 'The soils of the Weald'. *Proceedings of the Geologists' Association* 86(4): 593-610.

Markham, G. 1683. *The Inrichment of the Weald of Kent.* London: Hannah Sawbridge.

Martin, W.S., and B.P. Row. c.1897. *Tunbridge Wells of To-day.* London: Beechings Ltd.

Martynova, O.M. 1962. 'Otryad Neuroptera. Setchatokrylye'. In: Rodendorf, B.B. (ed.). *Osnovy Paleontologii: Chlenistonogie, Trakheinye i Khelitserovye.* Moskva: Akademii Nauk, S.S.S.R.

Tunbridge Wells and Rusthall Commons

Menuhin, D. 1984. *Fiddler's Moll.* London: Weidenfeld & Nicholson.
Pakaluk, J., and S.A. Slipinski. 1995. *Biology, Phylogeny, and Classification of Coleoptera.* Warszawa: Muzeum i Instytut Zoologii PAN.
Panfilov, D.V. 1968. 'Kalligrammatidy (Neuroptera, Kalligrammatidae) iz yurskikh otlozhenii Karatau'. In: Rodendorf, B.B. (ed.). *Yurskie nasekomye Karatau.* Moskva: Akademii Nauk, S.S.S.R.
Patmore, J.M. 1997. *High Weald Natural Area Profile.* Lewes: English Nature.
Pelton, R. 1871. *Pelton's Illustrated Guide to Tunbridge Wells and the Neighbouring Towns and Villages, with a Description of the Local Botany & Geology.* Tunbridge Wells: R. Pelton.
Pepys, S. Diary.
Philp, E.G. 1982. *Atlas of the Kent Flora.* Maidstone: Kent Field Club.
Philipot, T. 1776. *Villare Cantianium.* 2nd edition. Lynn.
Phippen, J. 1839 et seq. *Colbran's New Guide for Tunbridge Wells.* Tunbridge Wells: J. Colbran.
Robinson, D.A., and R.B.G. Williams. 1984. *Classic Landforms of the Weald. Landform Guides,* 4. Geographical Association.
Rowlands, M.L.J., and I.C. Beavis. 1991. *Tunbridge Wells in Old Photographs.* Stroud: Alan Sutton Publishing Ltd.
Rowlands, M.L.J., and I.C. Beavis. 1994. *Tunbridge Wells in Old Photographs – A Second Selection.* Stroud: Alan Sutton Publishing Ltd.
Rowzee, L. 1656. *The Queens Welles. That Is, A Treatise of the Nature and vertues of Tunbridge Water.* London.
Ruffell, A., A. Ross, and K. Taylor. 1996. *Early Cretaceous Environments of the Weald.* Geologists' Association Guide, 55.
Savidge, A. 1975. *Royal Tunbridge Wells.* Tunbridge Wells: Midas Books.
Shaw, W.A. 1906. *The Knights of England.* London: Sherratt & Hughes
Sprange, J. 1786. *The Tunbridge Wells Guide.* Tunbridge Wells: J. Sprange.
Walther, J. 1904. 'Die Fauna der Solnhofener Plattenkalke'. *Denkschriften der Medizinisch-Naturwissen-schaftlichen Gesellschaft zu Jena* 11: 133-214, pl. viii.
Webb, N. 1986. *Heathlands* (New Naturalist Series). London: Collins.
Witney, K.P. 1976. *The Jutish Forest – A Study of the Weald of Kent from 450 to 1380 A.D.* London: The Athlone Press.